THE "Nabes"

Toronto's wonderful neighbourhood movie houses

THE "Nabes"

Toronto's wonderful neighbourhood movie houses

JOHN SEBERT

Published by Mosaic Press, 1252 Speers Rd., Units 1 & 2, Oakville, ON L6L 5N9 Canada and Mosaic Press, 4500 Witmer Industrial Estates, PMB 145, Niagara Falls, NY 14305-1386

Design by Ken Rodmell
Production by Norton Hamill Design

National Library of Canada Cataloguing in Publication Data

Sebert, John, 1930-
    The "Nabes": Toronto's wonderful neighbourhood movie houses

ISBN 0-88962-770-3

Motion pictire theaters – Ontario – Toronto – Pictorial works. 2. Motion picture theatres – Ontario – Toronto – History. I. Jewison, Norman II. Title.

FC3097.63.S42 2001   791.43'09713'541   C2001-901932-7
F1059.5.T688A2 2001

The Canada Council | Le Conseil des Arts
for the Arts | du Canada

Mosaic Press acknowledges the assistance of the Canada Council and the Department of Canadian Heritage, Government of Canada, for the support of our publishing program.

ISBN 0-88962-770-3
Printed and bound in Canada

MOSAIC PRESS in Canada:
1252 Speers Rd., Units 1 & 2,
Oakville, ON L6L 5N9
Phone/FAX: 905 825-2130
mosaicpress@on.aibn.com

MOSAIC PRESS in US:
4500 Witmer Industrial Estates,
PMB 145, Niagara Falls, NY. 14305-1386
Phone/FAX: 1-800-387-8992
mosaicpress@on.aibn.com

Contents

Foreword by Elwy Yost vii

Famous Players ix

Acknowledgements x

Introduction 3

The "Nabes" by John Sebert 5

Northerners 19

Eastenders 35

Central 45

West End 61

The Danforth 77

St.Clair Area 89

College / Queen / Dundas West 101

Bloor–Bathurst 115

Almost Survivors 127

Reminiscences 131

Foreword by Elwy Yost

I feel honoured to be asked to write a foreword to this new book on the "Nabes", a tribute to the neighbourhood movie houses and the hardworking people who ran them in the hardest of times. It was at these theatres that I first began to love movies, which led to my being able to bring them to you for many years on TVO's Saturday Night at the Movies. This is a gallant project from some people who love the movies as much as I do. Here is a little reminiscence of my early movie going days.

By July of 1931, when I turned six, movies had learned how to talk, and the Fox Theatre on Main Street in the town of Weston, where I was born, started to become my own private Babylon.

My first experience was the Saturday matinee, which ran from 1:30 to 4:00 or 4:30, and cost me the dime Dad or Mom had given me, plus a cent for the little brown paper bag of candy I got in the lobby. Then it was into the theatre proper with 400 other kids, where I always sat well forward with chums from King Street Public School. Soon the lights started to dim and the stage curtains parted, and the screen and the sound system were suddenly alive with the "News of the Day".

Several selected shorts followed, including a chapter from a serial, 'The Galloping Ghost', starring Red Grange; a Popeye cartoon; an Edgar

Kennedy or Leon Errol comedy; and a double feature including Ken Maynard in 'Smoking Guns' and Tom Mix in 'Riders of Death Valley'.

Then home to tell Dad the plots of the two features while Mom made supper.

Sometimes, on the stage area in front of the screen, our theatre manager, Mr. Scott, would hold a yo-yo contest. I bravely entered a number of these, but alas, like Charlie Brown, I never won.

And then the time came when I was around 12, to say goodbye to Saturday matinees, and be allowed by Mom and Dad to go to the show at night. How well this 75-year-old mind can remember the sparkling white lights on the Fox Weston Theatre marquee as I approached its bright entrance, keenly looking forward to flying to Tibet with Ronald Colman and discovering the haunting mysteries of Shangri-La in 'Lost Horizon'.

One night when the first show had ended at 9:00 p.m.—-it was 'Tarzan and The Green Goddess'—-I remember being surprised in seeing Mr. Scott courteously escort my Dad to a chair in the back row. He had obviously driven down to give me a lift home, and the manager was rescuing him from standing out in the cold. While Dad had always loved movies in the 1920s, the Depression was making him feel that he couldn't afford to go. "Well", I thought, "it was high time Dad got to see a movie." So I slipped back into my seat and saw the Tarzan film all over again. Then I walked up the aisle and feigned real surprise at seeing Dad.

We never openly discussed the circumstances of that evening, but on the drive home Dad leaned over, clasped my hand, and whispered, "Thanks, Pal."

Famous Players

It is the magic of the movie theatre! Sitting in the dark with hundreds of strangers, quietly munching on popcorn while a story 10 times larger than life brightly unfolds in front of you, is something that touches nearly everybody. There is no other experience quite like it. For hours you can escape from all your problems and live in another world. Often one's fondest memories are associated with being inside a movie house.

When Famous Players Inc. was asked to support this book, there was never any question of our involvement. Since 1920, when our first theatre was opened, we have been offering families a unique entertainment destination, a place that both captivates and stimulates the imagination. We imagine that author/photographer John Sebert and all the contributors to this book would attest to this fact. Watching a movie, in what was considered at the time to be "state-of-the-art" movie houses, they all

would have come away with their own memories. We are grateful to John for his initiative and wonderful photo gathering, and all the writers for sharing their remembrances with us in this book.

Famous Players Inc. is proud to be associated with this fascinating project and congratulates John Sebert, Edgar Cowan, Mosaic Press and all the contributors to this important addition to the heritage archives of Toronto.

FAMOUS PLAYERS
Big Screen Big Sound Big Difference

Acknowledgements

**his book** is a very personal labour of love. As a youngster, I went to most of the movie houses photographed here, and most of the descriptions are from my memory. But memories are funny things—the mind plays tricks on us. I have cross-checked most facts, but I'm sure there may be some inaccuracies. For this I apologize.

I could not have accomplished this project without a lot of help from others.

I would like to acknowledge these people and sources. First of all, Edgar Cowan, without whom there would be no book.

Second, various archives that supplied many of the early theatre photographs and particularly, Andrew Roger of The National Archives, Ramonde Cadorette at the Archives of Ontario, and John Huzil at the City of Toronto Archives. Next, my old friend, Mandel Sprachman, whose expertise on theatres and their architecture helped immensely. Many thanks to Joe and Lila Strashin, again old friends, for taking us back to the Thirties and the Cameo Theatre. And to John Thompson, who came on board in an editing capacity, but provided much more, with photos and details of our "Nabes".

Also to all the Toronto notables who shared their reminiscences of their early love of our movie houses. And lastly to Adele, my wife, who as well as dotting the "i"s and crossing the "t"s, helped immensely with the project. A real romantic, she still has a cryptic message written by me on the back of an envelope from 35 years ago, "Meet you at the New Yorker, 14 rows from the back!"

John Sebert

nabe (nāb), *n.* Usually, **nabes**. *Slang.* a neighbourhood movie theater. [shortening and resp. of NEIGHBOURHOOD]

Random House Dictionary of English Language

Introduction

In the early 1950s, before the popularity of television, there were over 130 neighbourhood movie theatres in what was then a much smaller Toronto. With the exception of a handful of veritable palaces in the downtown core, they were scattered throughout the city, from the Beaches to the Junction, and north to the city limits. Some were owned by large corporations, but many were mom and pop operations serving their neighbourhood with a steady diet of "B" movies, re-runs and serials. These were the "Nabes".

Today in the age of suburbia and expressways, it's hard to imagine that movie going was a simple matter of walking a few blocks or hopping a streetcar to the theatre of one's choice. For some the preference was a western, for others the serials but for me it was *film noir*. Of course, no one called them *film noir* at the time, but their darkness of theme and appearance seemed to strike a chord in me. Today, after their beatification by the French critics, these same films of the 30s, 40s and 50s are recognized as a distinct and valuable part of cinema lore. At the time, however, these films were often considered the "B" movies. Sometimes they filled the lower half of double bills, and rarely played the large downtown first run theatres , and instead went directly to the "Nabes". For me, a kid growing up in Toronto's west end, these theatres included the Esquire, the Runnymede, the Beaver, the Apollo, the Blo-ordale and the Academy. As I grew older, my universe expanded to include such standbys as the Midtown, the Broadway, and the York. Today, none of these theatres exist. Some were totally razed, but many of the original buildings still stand, converted to a variety of uses. The Runnymede is now a Chapters bookstore, the Ace a drugstore, and the Adelphi, a church. A very few still operate as movie theatres serving film buffs with classic or cult films, while others cater to the distinctive cultural needs of some of Toronto's larger ethnic groups.

Although I no longer live in Toronto, my periodic forays into the city have often taken me to driving around the neighbourhoods of my youth. Often, in fits of curiosity or nostalgia, I've searched for the vestiges of those same movie houses I haunted in search of the elusive *film noir*. At some point, I decided to photograph these theatres as they exist today and this exercise became the inspiration for this book.

For those who remember this era and some of the theatres portrayed, I hope this book provides a link to a more innocent time. For others, it may represent yet another piece in the mosaic that is the history of the city of Toronto.

John Sebert
Port Hope, Ontario
August, 2001

"The Nabes" by John Sebert

Usually it's the grand palaces that are featured whenever the history of movie theatres from Hollywood's Golden Years is written about. In Toronto, that would mean the Imperial (Pantages), Loew's, and Shea's Hippodrome. It's time that we paid a little tribute to those independent theatres whose very existence depended on how many patrons entered their establishments. These "Nabes", or neighbourhood movie theatres, were a phenomenon that peaked in the late 1940s, then declined until becoming almost extinct by the 1970s. They served their purpose in their time, then disappeared. What happened? Why did a piece of our culture that was so popular fade into oblivion? People still go to movies in record numbers, Hollywood still grinds out as many films as ever, but times change.

The motion picture business in Toronto, as in other big cities, started and grew early in the 20th century. It was a novelty at first; people would pay simply to see a train move across a screen. The venue was simple, usually being a converted storefront, with a sheet pinned up on the back wall as a screen, and this lasted for about the first decade. The second decade witnessed the First World War, and a more sophisticated motion picture. Story lines crept into them, and writers, directors and actors from the stage began participating. The novelty was fading, people demanded to be entertained with more than just motion, and they wanted a story.

As the pictures became more sophisticated, so did the movie houses. The owners and managers felt that the audience would not be satisfied with just sitting in a dark room to see their presentations, so a new breed of theatre, something spectacular, was needed to attract the patrons into the movie house. This had first happened in the United States, particularly in New York and Chicago. Then, Toronto was infiltrated by a group of entrepreneurial Americans who came, raised money, and built our first film palaces. The Allen family, from Pennsylvania, built about a dozen of these lavish theatres around the city. These included the Century, the Beach, the Parkdale and the College. The theatres were so lavish that they had bankrupted the Allens by 1923. The first glimmer of today's Famous Players appeared when another young American, Nat Nathenson, tired of the amusement park business, talked some local high rollers, notably E.L.Ruddy of billboard fame, into buying the old Ambrose Small Grand Opera House on Adelaide Street West. It was converted into the Regent movie house. At about this time, the early 1920s, movies improved. Editing was now improved, better writers were hired to write the screenplays, and equipment was upgraded. It was apparent now that patrons were paying to see the picture, regardless of how awesome the theatre was. There would always be a place for the big, lavish, first run theatres, but now, with more movies being produced on smaller budgets, there was room for a new category of movie house. Thus the neighbourhood movie theatres, or what the trade called the "Nabes", were born. These varied from mom and pop storefront conversions to inexpensive, purpose-built auditoriums.

These "Nabes" sprouted up all over Toronto, forcing some of the grander theatres to become second run "Nabes". The less ostentatious houses became known as third run or "subsequent" houses.

The motion picture business doesn't seem complicated. Producers, e.g. Paramount Pictures, make the movies and theatres exhibit them. However, there are various complications along the way. There are the distributors who rent the movies from the producers, and they are sometimes affiliated with them. In the past, these affiliations frequently applied to a group of theatres called circuits; practically every "Nabe" belonged to a circuit. The three big circuits in Toronto were Famous Players, B&F, and 20th Century, followed later by Odeon. The independently owned theatres banded together in their own circuits to obtain a better deal from the distributor, using their combined buying power to book films. These circuits were Allied, Premier, Associated and Independent. Lastly, there were two other types of theatres: the indy owner who joined the bigger circuit or chain (i.e. B&F or 20th Century); and the low men on the totem pole, the truly independent theatre owners such as Nathan Cohen of the Avon,(nee King's Playhouse), on Queen Street West, and J.B.Goldhar of the Paramount on St. Clair Avenue West. They had to book their films from what remained after the "biggies" had made their choices. The pickings weren't that good for current films, but could be turned into an advantage by judicious booking of classic films. We see the Apollo screening 'Gunga Din' in 1943, four years after it was released.

With the 1930s came the Depression and hard times. Many people were out of work, or with much reduced wages. The movie houses became the big escape: entertainment for the masses. The inexpensive neighbourhood theatre was the natural venue. Prices dropped dramatically, from $1.00 admission in the 1920s to 35 cents by 1935, with the cheap seats, usually on the side aisles, going for 20 cents. Kids paid five cents for the Saturday matinee. In 1939 it was quite a shock when the government added a war tax and the price went up to six cents. At the same time, Hollywood, and to a lesser degree London, was turning out a better product. People were flocking to the theatres, so much so that the managers could afford to have two or even three complete changes a week. And, this was in the days of the double bill, with cartoons and shorts thrown in.

The "Nabes" evolved because they became established in specific neighbourhoods. Their customers came from the neighbourhood. You usually walked to the theatre, and very seldom went to one outside your own neighbourhoood. This made the manager a very important person locally. His main job, of course, was to get people into his theatre by promoting it visibly, and by doing this he became a local public figure. Part lawyer, confessor, policeman, banker and often baby sitter, he was often referred to as the mayor of the district. Indeed Don Summerville, manager of the Prince of Wales on the Danforth, became so good at it he actually became Mayor of Toronto.

It is interesting when looking at the locations of these theatres to see that many were located in concentrated pockets. On College Street, west of Spadina, there were seven: the Garden at 290, the

Melody at 346, the Bellevue at 360, the King at 565, the Pylon at 606, the Monarch at 720, and the College at 960. Another grouping around Bloor and Bathurst comprised: the Bloor, the Midtown, the Alhambra, the Metro, the Kenwood, the Paradise and the Doric. Other groupings could be found in the Junction and on lower Parliament Street. An anthropologist could probably make a lot out of the fact that none of these districts were even middle class at the time.

So what happened to all our neighbourhood movie houses? Obviously TV's arrival in the early 1950s changed our entertainment habits. People got used to watching movies in their living rooms. But there were other factors that went against the "Nabes". New techniques were introduced by Hollywood to combat the upstart television industry, such as wide screen, and stereo sound. Converting to these technologies would have been a major expense to a small theatre, so few switched over. Most were left lagging even further behind the majors with their new toys. Another cultural fact was that postwar theatre patrons were becoming mobile. They were buying cars, and finding a place to park at your friendly "Nabe" could be a problem.

Then, as though the competition of Famous Players wasn't enough, J. Arthur Rank brought his giant Odeon chain of first run houses to Toronto immediately after the war. Odeon peppered the city with elegant, large theatres. The final nail in the coffin for any "Nabe" that was lucky enough to still exist, was the introduction of the multiplexes in the 1970s. That did it!

Helen McNamara, in a 1969 Telegram article titled "Your Friendly Nabe, We Get By, But There's No Fortune in This Business Anymore", wrote about the decline of the local movie house. She quoted Mort Margolius, manager of the College Theatre at College and Dovercourt, a landmark for over 50 years, "I don't think people understand that a city is not a city, it's a series of small towns." His neighbourhood was working class. During World War Two, when the defense plants operated south on King Street, almost everybody in the family had a job, even Grandma, and almost everybody went to the movies.

Helen goes on to describe an incident that Margolius had to cope with. Queen Juliana and Prince Bernhardt of the Netherlands were taking refuge in Canada during the war. Their attaché called Mort up, saying that the Queen wanted to see 'The Great Lie', starring Bette Davis, which was showing at the College. "No problem", said Mort. When the royal couple arrived at the theatre they insisted on buying their own tickets, as they wished to remain incognito, and Mort was happy to comply. Unfortunately, the attaché bought 25 cent tickets, but they mistakenly sat in the 35 cent section. An usher, not realizing there was royalty in the house, made them move to the cheaper seats. At this point, with all the ruckus, their cover was blown when a Dutch lady in the audience recognized them. Soon the entire theatre was abuzz with the news. Margolius was always known as "The Chief" to the citizens of the College/Dovercourt area, in part because of his ability to control the Roxton gang of teenagers before the war, and the notorious Beanery gang after the war. Wearing another hat, on Sundays, he turned the College into a church for returning veterans who needed a place to worship. Margolius was the epitome of the 'public character' who keeps the inner city working, whom Jane Jacobs cited in her book "The Death and Life of Great American Cities."

Another manager that Helen McNamara mentioned was Harry Sherman of the Fox, a 500-seat theatre out near the end of the Queen streetcar line. Sherman was manager for 18 of his 38 years in the movie theatre business. He told her of the history of the Fox. It was built for $15,000 and opened in October 1913 as " the theatre without a name". This bit of cleverness didn't last too long, and it soon was called the Pastime. Arthur Webster then took it over and, in a patriotic moment, changed the name to the Prince Edward (another theatre was called the Prince of Wales). When Prince Edward abdicated the British throne, this was too much for Webster and his son Cecil, who was then running the theatre. They changed the name, yet again, to the Fox, which it remains today. Part of its longevity is attributed to Harry Sherman's success as manager in the 1950s, when "Nabes" were falling by the wayside. Sherman knew his audience; instead of catering to a youthful clientele, he served his middle-aged patrons. They were very choosy; they wanted first class pictures, or they wouldn't come. To keep expenses down, Sherman did his own buying and booking. He said "even in a small theatre like the Fox, we still need six employees: a doorman, an usher, a cashier, a cleaner, a projectionist and a girl on the candy counter." McNamara ends her story with the title, a quote from Sherman: "We get by, but there's no fortune in this business anymore."

The current owners of the Fox concur, "things haven't changed much in the ensuing 32 years." But Tom Litvinskas and Jerry Szczur "love the biz! Why else would we work so hard in this crazy business?" Twenty-eight years ago, these boyhood friends started what is now the Festival Cinemas, Toronto's only remaining circuit of neighbourhood theatres. They were film buffs, barely out of their teens, who would scour the city for interesting movies. The partners admired the moxie and groundbreaking policy of the Roxy on the Danforth, which charged 99 cents to see a wide variety of movies. Tom and Jerry spent many hours in Parkdale's Kum-C. When their local "Nabe", the Kingsway, became dark and was up for rent, they, along with several friends, decided to get into the movie business. They thought, "What's the big deal? You show a picture, people line up and buy tickets to get in." Some 30 years later, Tom and Jerry have a circuit of six local theatres: the Kingsway, Paradise, Fox, Royal, Music Hall (Century) and the Revue, all running seven nights a week. They were also involved with many other theatres over the years. The reason for their success is their hands-on approach. Tom and Jerry have been responsible for upgrading equipment, renovating the theatres, booking films, doing the books and hiring staff (as in 1969, a theatre still requires six people). Tom says "that old adage that you don't make money on the pictures, you make it on the popcorn, is still true. The multiplexes make more money because they charge more for their popcorn". Certainly, if it weren't for Tom and Jerry, Toronto would have lost six more theatres, or about 50% of the remaining working "Nabes".

Another manager whose whole career was spent in the movie business was Wannie Tyers. He ended his days as Advertising Manager for the Odeon chain. Wannie cut his teeth in the out-of-town circuits, managing theatres in Dunnville and St. Thomas. He proved so adept at his job that Famous Players brought him to Toronto, where he managed, with great success, their prestigious Runnymede and Village Theatres. His expertise was in organizing imaginative promotions to publicize the current picture. Wannie reminisced about the line of fire trucks outside his theatre that he arranged for when an 'inferno' type picture was showing inside. Wannie's life-long dream, never fulfilled, was to own the wonderful Village Theatre.

A much-loved and respected pioneer manager, whose whole family seemed to be in the theatre business, was George Lester. He ran the King Theatre after operating the Royal, which he started in 1915. The Royal was very primitive, with about 200 wooden chairs screwed to the wooden floor. His family moved into a flat above the auditorium and worked downstairs in the theatre. Lester then opened the King, across the road on College Street, in 1926. His son Lionel worked part-time at the King, which survived with a name change, becoming the Studio, one of the city's first art houses. After a career in the film distribution business, Lionel, with his brother Bob, operated this theatre from 1953 up until the 1970s, when it finally closed. George Lester was an institution on College Street. The King was so successful that in 1933 the manager of the nearby Duchess Theatre on Dundas Street was arrested for hiring two strong-arm thugs from Detroit to beat up the unsuspecting Lester. The thugs, when apprehended, spilled the beans on the hapless manager.

If George Lester was an institution, then the Lester Family was a small dynasty. Sons Lionel and Bob, as mentioned, worked at the Studio; a brother-in-law, Abe Polakoff, managed the Park (Lansdowne); brother

Sam ran the Doric at Bloor and Gladstone; another brother, Harry, operated the Bonita on Gerrard Street. When asked if his grandfather, George Angel Lester, had left any pictures or memorabilia of his King Theatre, publisher Malcolm Lester pointed out that the movie business was, to his grandfather, a business, not an artistic endeavour, so why would he have left any frivolous memorabilia around? Malcolm said that the theatre business was one of the few businesses that a Jewish immigrant could successfully get into in "Toronto, The Good" in the Twenties and Thirties. Therefore, a large number of theatre owners and managers were from such families.

An excellent example of this endeavour was the Strashin family, of the Cameo Theatre. Bertha and Sam Strashin owned a variety store on Kingston Road in the early 1930s, and lived nearby. Bertha, the visionary of the family, decided it was time (1934) to get into show business. They had five children, so this was quite a gamble. The Strashins sold the store and looked around for an ideal location for their proposed theatre. They found an empty lot on the east side of Pape Ave., a few blocks north of the Danforth. The Strashins then talked to Abe Sprachman, of theatre architects Kaplan & Sprachman. The cost of the new theatre would be $85,000, total. Sam was reluctant, as they only had been able to raise $5,000, but Bertha had a vision, one similar to W.P. Kinsella's 'A Field Of Dreams'; "If we build it, they will come!" Therefore, the plans went ahead, mortgages were put in place, and in April 1934, the very depth of the Depression, the foundation was dug. The Strashins named the theatre the Cameo; it sounded classy and would look good on the marquee. The Cameo opened in November 1934, with 'The Thin Man' as its first feature.

The plans for the theatre included an apartment upstairs for the Strashins' son Jack, who was the projectionist, and his wife Kay, who ran the confectionery store that was built into the front facade. Business started slowly, but Sam ran a tight ship; he had many promotions such as 'Free Dishes' on Tuesdays and 'Foto-Nite' on Wednesdays, which traditionally were slow nights. Lila Strashin, a daughter-in-law, remembers stocking her first kitchen with 'movie dishes'. Soon, things began to roll. On many nights near-capacity crowds filled the 750 seats and, at 25 cents a head, real money could be made. The family moved to a better part of town. One son, Sam Jr., entered law school, and a younger son, Israel, who worked nights as an usher, became a doctor.

The movie business flourished during the Second World War. Hollywood was turning out a record number of films. Theatres were falling over each other with promotions, vying for customers with two, even three complete changes a week, and at least two shows a night. However, by the mid-1950s, things were not looking so good. At first, there were a few empty seats, then, a half-empty house. People were staying home to watch the new novelty, television. The alarm sounded. Finally the Strashins saw that only a few patrons were showing up. The handwriting was on the wall; TV had killed the golden goose. Eventually, in 1957, the Strashins, after 23 good years, decided it was time to sell up. The building was sold to Loblaws, who transformed it into a supermarket, then finally sold it to its present owners, Canada Trust. Over the years, the Cameo had been good to the Strashins.

Another offshoot of these managers, and sometimes even a more important figure, was the cashier or ticket seller out front in the box office, a term that has come to describe the viability of the whole theatre business. She was usually a stern, gray haired matron who knew the district and everybody in it, and knew when you graduated from child to adult. It was a plus to be considered an adult when hoping to con your way into a movie house's evening performance, but a minus at the matinee if one was hoping for a child's' 10 cent ticket. The well-known lady at the Runnymede was credited with knowing every youngster's birth date in the district. Joseph Mitchell, in a 1940 New Yorker story, characterized one such cashier perfectly. "She sits in the cage, profoundly uninterested in moving pictures, like a Queen, wearing a green celluloid eye shade." The box office, no bigger than a telephone booth, was her domain. She took no nonsense from the kids, but was known to pass out jawbreakers to the younger ones. She never seemed to watch a movie, but was the critic to ask if in doubt as to the merits of the program. Quite often, in the family owned theatre, Mother was in the box office.

The movie exhibition houses have varied greatly, from the "black top" tent shows on fair grounds, to today's "spaceship" architecture multiplexes. We started with the nickelodeon, which was usually a converted storefront. Then the American entrepreneurs, such as Marcus Loew, introduced Toronto to the palatial Adam Revival style of Thomas Lamb, theatre architect extraordinaire. Next, the Allens brought in C. Howard Crane to design his Beaux-Arts and Empire styled theatres. The common denominator was decorating with painted, formed plaster and lath to achieve rococo embellishments. These looked lavish and costly, but were quite cheap to produce. This décor gave the palaces a look that seemed much more expensive than actually was the case. It was the architecture of illusion, just like the movies shown inside.

By the time the Depression hit, the theatre business had experienced Louis XVI, Baroque, Romanesque, Atmospheric and Art Nouveau architecture; however, with the faltering economy, patrons rebelled at the excesses. They wanted cheap movies in a simple, austere auditorium, and they got what they asked for, Art Deco. This style was also called Streamline Moderne, and it suited the Depression to a "T". It was a no-nonsense architectural style that became the look of practically every "Nabe" built during the 1930s. Chrome and mirrors replaced stylized columns and floral ceilings. Movie theatres started looking like airports, banks and schools. These functional movie houses were almost all designed by the new theatre experts, the Toronto partners of Kaplan and Sprachman, whose crowning achievement was the 1936 Eglinton Theatre. Good examples of this style and Kaplan and Sprachman's designs were the Bloordale, Cameo, Bayview, and Bellevue.

By 1939, the building of movie theatres had almost ground to a halt, with just a few being built in the year prior to the war. Mandel Sprachman, who would himself become a noted Toronto theatre architect, was just 14 years old at the time. He remembers his father, Abe, the architect, doing a jig around the kitchen table after returning from a meeting with Nat Nathanson. He had learned of the prospect of designing 50 theatres for a new entity, Canadian Odeon Theatres. Alas, fate intervened, and six years of war put those plans on hold. When Odeon finally did come to Toronto, they built fewer but more lavish theatres in the four corners of Toronto. This started a trend to more centralized moviegoing, which would lead to the multiplexes with their ample parking. This competition, and the fact that TV was keeping people at home, meant that the need for "Nabes" had disappeared, and they mostly faded from view.

Northeners

This cluster of "Nabes" is, apart from those on Parliament Street, the only group situated mainly on Toronto's north- south streets. They included mostly theatres on Yonge St., Spadina Rd., Mount Pleasant Rd. and Bayview Ave., with two just off Avenue Rd. These theatres, located in a more affluent district, were better appointed and featured more first and second run films.

Oriole (International) Cinema (1941) *2061 Yonge St., east side, at Manor Rd.*

As an independently owned theatre in the 1920s, the Oriole's great location assured success. In 1942, it was taken over by 20th Century Theatres and, with great fanfare, the name changed to the Cinema. The theatre was upgraded to second run, at par with the Midtown. After the war, the former Oriole was closed for a renovation, and in 1949 opened as the International Cinema. It became, with its opulent sister theatre, the Towne Cinema, Toronto's first run foreign film theatre. These both remained successful, under direct control of Nat Taylor's wife Yvonne, well into the 1980s.

City of Toronto Archives: SC. 488-6056 / Archives of Ontario: RG.56-11/6.25

Bayview (1942) *605 Bayview Ave., east side, in the heart of Leaside*

It was built in 1936, as another Kaplan and Sprachman Art Deco theatre. The Bayview was a favourite 20th Century theatre that has become a grocery store after a losing battle to remain a live theatre. Although in a good location and a beautiful theatre, the Bayview was never a successful business.

Archives of Ontario: RG56-11 /5.5

Circle (1946) *2567 Yonge St., east side, north of Sherwood Ave.*

An institution in North Toronto, it was an early design of Kaplan and Sprachman, built in 1932. An independent "Nabe", the Circle became one of the main theatres in the 20th Century chain, when it was formed in 1943. It was one of the first Toronto theatres to provide a parking lot adjacent to the theatre. Interestingly, the Circle shoe store survives a few doors to the north.

National Archives of Canada: MISA 4561-8.

Eglinton (1947) *402 Eglinton Ave. West, north side, west of Avenue Rd.*

Famous Players should be proud of this gorgeous, 1930s-style movie house, designed in 1934 by Kaplan & Sprachman, and opened in 1936. It has withstood the test of time, with many restorations and improvements. Theatre buffs come from all over the world to study this museum-quality movie house.

Archives of Ontario: RG 56-11 /6.18

Hollywood (1946) *1519 Yonge St, east side, north of St.Clair Ave.*

This was the most important theatre left in the Allens' Premier group, in what had always been an upscale neighbourhood. It was their flagship, showing first and second run pictures. Shortly after this picture was taken, a second auditorium was built in the parking lot, making the Hollywood Toronto's first multi-screen theatre. It was long-lived, lasting until demolition in the millenium. Architecturally, the Hollywood was an Atmospheric, but for most of its life, the atmosphere was hidden with heavy drapes.

Archives of Ontario: RG 56-11/ 6.24—1950—City of Toronto Archives: SC 303-A

Glendale (1950) *1661 Avenue Road, east side, at Brookdale Ave.*

The Glendale, opened in 1950, was one of the last "Nabes", built under the 20th Century ownership. Located six blocks north of Lawrence Avenue, it served a newer area of numerous postwar houses. Patrons were greeted by a spacious lobby, and an auditorium that offered tiered (amphitheatre style) seating where the balcony blended down into the orchestra. Many people will remember the Glendale as the theatre where they saw the science fiction spectacular '2001: A Space Odyssey', during its lengthy run there. This was possible because of its state of the art sound and projection system, unique to the Glendale. The theatre closed on a high note after hosting the 1974 hit ' The Godfather, Part Two'. The Glendale site is occupied now by a car dealership.

City of Toronto Archives: SC.488-7344

For a long time, it was the flagship of second run theatres for Famous Players in North Toronto. Like the Runnymede on Bloor St. West, the Capitol was an important building. It remained a theatre until recently, then was converted to an upscale rental hall. This is an example of good adaptive reuse of a building.

Capitol (1938) *2492 Yonge St., west side, north of Castlefield Ave.*

Another 1940s glass-brick modern theatre, such as we saw being built in the new suburbs around the city. This gave Willowdale Toronto's first movie house north of the old city limits. It was a fairly large, 1000-seat theatre, and one of the last built by the Allens' Premier chain.

Archives of Ontario: RG-11-0-328-2

Willow (1948) 5269 Yonge Street, east side, between Sheppard and Finch

Belsize (1943) *551 Mount Pleasant Rd., east side, north of Davisville Ave.*

It was built in 1927, designed by architect Murray Brown, when some theatres combined live entertainment with movies. This enabled the Belsize to become the Crest in the 1950s, Toronto's legitimate theatre second only to the Royal Alexandra. It is a survivor, and, as the Regent, is still a neighbourhood movie house. The former Belsize has been designated a Heritage Property.

Archives of Ontario: RG56-11/6.19

Avenue (1952) *331 Eglinton Ave. West, south side, west of Avenue Rd.*

Built in 1937, across the street from the successful Eglinton Theatre, it was an independent that never reached its potential. Two years after opening, it was taken over by Ray Lewis as company for her newly-built Pylon Theatre. But even Lewis couldn't make the Avenue work, and during the war the Avenue became part of Famous Players, owners of the Eglinton Theatre. Towards the end of its career, the Avenue became the home of "Spring Thaw", Toronto's long-running yearly satirical revue.

City of Toronto Archives: RG 32A-392

Park (Bedford) (1950) *3291 Yonge St., east side, south of Glenforest Rd.*

As the Bedford, it was Famous Players' popular North Toronto theatre during the 1930s. It ended its days with the 20th Century group, after a makeover in the 1940s. The old auditorium now houses Storkland. The pitched roof of the old Bedford is still apparent in the contemporary photograph. The Park was one of the few examples of architect Murray Brown's theatre work in Toronto. It was originally built in 1929, but had a major renovation and name change to the Park in 1948.

Archives of Ontario: RG 56-11/6.42

Nortown (1949) *875 Eglinton Ave. West, south side, west of Bathurst Street.*

Probably the last single screen theatre built in Toronto by Famous Players. Along with the Village on Spadina Rd., the Nortown drew its patrons from the affluent Forest Hill neighbourhood, and its design and decoration reflected this. This was a high-end "Nabe".

City of Toronto Archives: SC.488-7342.

Fairlawn (1984) *3320 Yonge St., west side at Fairlawn Ave.*

In 1946, Odeon Theatres built three neighbourhood movie houses in Toronto: the Danforth, the Humber and this theatre, the Fairlawn. All large, (about 1200 seat houses), and opulent, they were instant hits. They introduced Toronto moviegoers to British films, loosening the stranglehold Hollywood had on our filmgoing habits. The Fairlawn introduced several innovations, one of which, the Saturday Morning Movie Club, was extremely popular with kids. It was treated like a mini film festival, with an emcee, usually the manager, introducing the upcoming film to the audience. Then in the 1960s, following the convention of most large theatres, it was twinned into two auditoriums. About the same time, the façade received a face-lift and it lost its marquee. The Fairlawn lasted well into the 1980s, finally closing its doors December 31, 1985.

Photo: John Thompson

East Enders

As Toronto moved further east along the lake, the population grew as well. Neighbourhoods such as Monarch Park, Greenwood, Kew Beach and Victoria Park attracted residents who, from the 1930s through the war years, supported their many local theatres.

Joy (1948) *1130 Queen St. East, north side, near Jones Ave.*

This tiny, 380-seat theatre was so small it didn't advertise. The Joy would subscribe to other Allied promotions, such as 'Foto-Nite' and dinnerware giveaways, to keep its customers loyal. It looked very much like the Vogue Theatre down the street at 1574 Queen St. East. When the Joy dropped its original name, the Rex, the owners were hard put to find another three-letter word to fit the marquee.

City of Toronto Archives: SC.257-464.

Eastwood (1948) *1430 Gerrard St. East, north side, west of Coxwell Ave.*

An 850-seat house in the B&F chain, it was the largest in a group of six theatres between Coxwell and Broadview. Its Beaux-Arts design facilitated its transformation into The India Centre. The Eastwood was run by Bill Summerville, whose brother Don not only managed the Prince of Wales theatre, but also became Mayor of Toronto.

Archives of Ontario: RG 56-11/6.17

Scarboro (1937) *960 Kingston Rd., north side, west of Bingham Ave.*

An Art Deco theatre built as a B&F theatre in 1936, it had 700 seats. As a promotion in 1940, you could win silverware and a volume of the American Encyclopedia by attending a movie. The original façade has endured through the former Scarboro's present use as a sportsbar.

City of Toronto Archives: SC.488-1128

Birchcliff (1950) *1485 Kingston Rd., south side, east of Warden Ave.*

As the city expanded farther east after the war, the movie houses followed. This 20th Century theatre served the Scarborough crowd. As a suburban theatre it had that "ranch style" look that was so prevalent in postwar Toronto's outskirts. Interestingly, the Birchcliff's site was formerly occupied by a streetcar barn.

Archives of Ontario: RG-11-0-272-1

Beach (1940) *1971 Queen St. East, south side, east of Woodbine Ave.*

In the heart of the Beaches, this Famous Players theatre, with 1300 seats, was the largest in the area. It was built with its twins, the Parkdale and the St. Clair, in 1921, and lasted into the 1970s, after which all three were turned into mini-malls. This was possible because of their unique construction, with the long side of the building fronted on the street.

National Archives of Canada: PA111060

Guild (1937) *1275 Gerrard St. East, south side, at Greenwood Ave.*

An institution in the east end, and originally called the Greenwood, the Guild was one of nine independents that joined forces in 1943 to form the Allied Theatre Group. This became the strongest organization representing independent owners. Like many other movie houses, the Guild was next door to a United Cigar Store and a five cent hamburger stand.

City of Toronto Archives: SC488-1123

Family (1935) *2173 Queen St.East, south side, at Kew Gardens*

A very early "Nabe", the Family was built in 1914. After World War Two, it was renamed the Lake, not surprisingly, as it was in the centre of the Beaches, and within a stones throw of Lake Ontario. The Beaches district was well served in the very early years by three movie houses. Known as "The Home Of Ideal Entertainment", the Family Theatre was eventually replaced by a Royal Bank. It was in this theatre that a pre-teen Norman Jewison learned to love movies.

City of Toronto Archives: SC 488-2782

Fox (2000) *2236 Queen St. East, east of Beech Ave., north side.*

What a history this little (550-seat) theatre has had. A. B. Webster opened the theatre in 1914 as "The Theatre Without A Name", then held a name-the-theatre contest, with the Pastime winning out. This only lasted one year. During World War One, as a patriotic gesture, the two-year-old theatre received its third name, the Prince Edward, named for the man who would be King. When he didn't become King and abdicated instead, this proved too much for the Websters, who then made a last name change to the Fox, which it has remained for the past 63 years. Although the entrance faced Queen Street, the auditorium actually ran along Queen Street behind a series of storefronts. It is still a movie house, owned and run as part of the Festival chain, which purchased it in 1978.

Photo: John Thompson

Central

These were the downtown theatres. Many of them had to compete with the palaces on Yonge Street. Some were of the three features a day, open all night variety. The Casino and Victory were famous (or infamous) for their girlie strip shows as well as movies. It's hard to imagine how one street, Parliament, warranted so many "Nabes". The residential area east from the once grand Jarvis Street to Riverdale Park was in the 1930s a high-density working class neigh-bourhood. These people craved their movies and kept the theatres busy. Most of these establishments are gone now, except for the Embassy, now the New Yorker, a legitimate theatre.

Broadway & Casino *75 and 87 Queen St West, south side, west of Bay St.*

The Broadway, originally the Globe, had an interesting life. Later, as the Roxy, it was Toronto's first burlesque house, with "Girlie" shows and movies. In 1935, the manager was murdered in his office and his son-in law, Murray Little, took over the management. When the Allens decided to move into the burlesque business a year later, with a design of Kaplan & Sprachman, they built the Casino Theatre five doors to the west. Little then formed a partnership with the Allens, and ran the Casino until it was closed in 1963. The Roxy became the Broadway, and, as well as becoming a three features a day house, its sign shop above the theatre was used as a rehearsal hall for the Casino chorus girls. The Casino, as a house-clearing ploy, ran inexpensive movies between stage shows; many of these have turned up as classic "Film Noirs".

City of Toronto Archives: SC 488-1143: York University Archives: 1974-002/046

Arcadian (1949) *10 Queen St. East, north side, east of Yonge St.*

It's amazing how some of our theatres remain in our memories, and some disappear. The Arcadian is certainly one of the latter. It was in the shadow of both Eatons and Simpsons, but hardly anyone remembers the theatre. Its name was the same as Simpsons famous dining room. The Arcadian was a storefront theatre, located on the main floor of an office building. In the 1960s its neighbour was the famous Town Tavern. The Arcadian was originally called the Variety, and was one of the first Toronto movie houses to specialize in foreign films. The façade of the early bank building next door is being preserved as part of a new complex. It's wishful thinking, but perhaps it will include a little theatre named the Arcadian.

City of Toronto Archives: SC.-488-6854-3

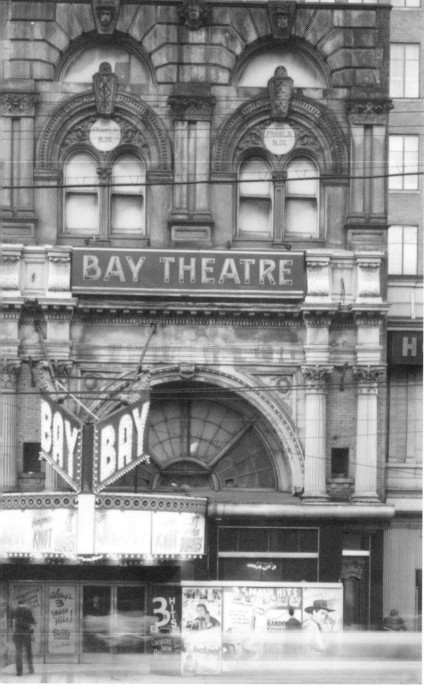

A very strange movie house. It opened in 1919 as the Colonial Theatre in the Franklin Building. Although it lasted until 1965, when the Simpson Tower was built in its place, hardly anyone remembers the Bay, even though the theatre stood out like a sore thumb. The façade was resurrected from the demolished Customs House on Front Street. The interior consisted of a series of wrought iron balconies reminiscent of a small Eiffel Tower. In its final days the Bay became a "Three Hits a Day" show. Its neighbour to the west was a Toronto landmark, Bowles Lunch, and to the east was another forgotten theatre, the Photodrome. It was best known as the Ace in its glory years. When the Ace name moved up to the Danforth, they literally moved the marquee sign, name and all.

U of Calgary Architectural
Archives: Pan. 55175 –9

Bay (1955) *43 Queen St. West, across from the old City Hall*

An independent neighbour to the Bluebell, it was a bustling theatre, but fell prey to post-war urban renewal with the building of Regent Park. An absolutely typical, purpose-built "Nabe".

City of Toronto Archives: RG 8-41/80

Eclipse (1948) *387 Parliament St., east side, south of Dundas St.*

Victory (1942) 287 Spadina Ave., east side, northeast corner of Dundas

The Victory Theatre was built in 1922 as the Standard Theatre. It replaced the demolished National, the home of Yiddish theatre. Yiddish theatre flourished at the Standard until 1935 when the name was changed to the Strand. An independent group introduced an American film policy that eventually failed for lack of product. The 20th Century chain took over in 1940. They renovated the theatre and renamed it the Victory, which operated until neighbourhood attendance fell off. Leased to a group who ran burlesque strip shows, this new policy shook life into the old theatre. When attendance softened, a Chinese group bought the theatre, made major alterations, renamed it the Golden Harvest Theatre, and reopened it with Chinese films and live entertainment.

City of Toronto Archives: SC.488-6047.

Astor (Embassy) (1950) *651 Yonge St, east side, below Bloor St.*

It started life in the early 1930s as the Embassy, a theatre converted from an early Toronto building. Then, after being taken over by the 20th Century chain in 1950, it became the Astor. The building still had several more lives to live. When the neighbourhood movie business declined, the theatre was taken over by Bennet Fode of the Christie Theatre, who successfully changed the Astor into the New Yorker, an art house. Long after its motion picture days have passed, the New Yorker is still running as a legitimate theatre.

Archives of Ontario. AO-2126

National Archives of Canada MISA 4562-25

This was a large, 1000-seat house in the B&F Group, built in the 1920s. It, ironically, became one of CBC TV's television studios. The building remains today as a dance studio.

Archives of Ontario: RG 56-11/6.6

Carlton (1947) *509 Parliament St., east side, north of Carlton St.*

Teck (1932) *700 Queen St. East, north side, west of Broadview Ave.*

Bluebell (1947) *309 Parliament St., east side, south of Queen St.*

An old, silent movie house that hung on until the 1980s. The Bluebell was a very popular theatre in its day. The neighbourhood, in its heyday, was a quite respectable working class area whose inhabitants supported their theatre. After the war the Bluebell became the Gay, (the word had a more innocent meaning in those days), ultimately specializing in East Indian films. After showing second run American movies for most of its career, the condemned auditorium was replaced with a Quonset hut. Gentrified town houses now occupy the space.

Archives of Ontario: RG56-11/6.21

Regent (1938) *225 Queen St. East, south side, near Sherbourne St.*

There have been three Regent Theatres in Toronto's history. The first was the notorious Ambrose Small's Majestic Theatre on Adelaide St. West. It became the Regent after being taken over by Nat Nathanson, who formed what was to become Famous Players. The second, pictured here, was a small, 530-seat independent. The third is what the Crest has evolved back into, a neighbourhood movie house. This theatre had been around since World War One and was originally called the Moss Park.

City of Toronto Archives: SC.488-1141

Uptown (1936) *764 Yonge St., west side, south of Bloor.*

A huge theatre of 2800 seats, it was not exactly a neighbourhood theatre, but treated as one by the north of Bloor residents (who actually had their own theatre, the Rosedale, at 805 Yonge St. until the early 1930s). The Uptown, built by Loews in 1922, and subsequently taken over by Famous Players, was the first Toronto movie house equipped for sound. Although the main entrance was on Yonge Street, the bulk of the theatre faced on the less expensive back street, Balmuto, where there was a unique backdoor entrance. In the 1930s, the manager was Jack Arthur of CNE fame; thus, the Uptown became famous for its stage shows that accompanied the movies.

Mandel Sprachman Archives

Rio (1948) *373 Yonge St., east side, below Gerrard St.*

This tiny, 500-seat theatre filled the downtown gap for third run films. Surrounded by large movie houses, it existed longer than many of its more prestigious neighbours. For years, as the independent National, it boasted 20-cent adult admission. After the switch to Allied theatres and a name change in 1943 to Rio (commonly known to regulars as the "RTen"), it eventually became a "three to five features a day" movie house, well patronized by nearby Ryerson students.

Archives of Ontario: RG.56-11/6.46

La Plaza (1948) *735 Queen St. East, south side, east of Broadview*

A classic 1920s neighbourhood theatre, built for movies and legitimate plays, which is one reason it is still in use as "The Opera House" today. The theatre has really changed very little since it was built, providing Queen Street East with its own community theatre. In its heyday, the La Plaza was part of the B&F group.

Archives of Ontario: RG.-56-11-0-279-10

We find a host of "Nabes" way out at the west end of the city past Roncesvalles Ave., the unofficial western boundary of old Toronto. Many were built after the sound era arrived circa 1928. The theatres, which were a bit more modern and comfortable, were built to support the westerly-moving neighbourhood moviegoers. This group also included those in the important Junction area, a blue-collar district whose confines included the huge stockyards and packers, and also the two West Toronto railway stations.

Revue (1942) *400 Roncesvalles Ave., west side, south of Howard Park Ave.*

Another survivor in the Festival group, it looks pretty much today as when it opened in the 1920s. The theatre was part of the Associated (later 20th Century) group in the early 1930s. It has the distinction of being the longest running movie house with exactly the same facade that it opened with, in the teens.

Archives of Ontario: RG 56–1–6.45

State (Bloordale) (1951) *1606 Bloor St. West, north side, west of Dundas.*

A mid-1930s Art Deco house, one of the approximately 35 Bloor and Danforth theatres. It was another Kaplan & Sprachman design, so typical of the period. Although a well-thought-out movie house, the theatre never reached its potential, as it was on the fringe of about five neighbourhoods, but part of none. It finished its days as the State. Some theatre owners were not averse to duplicating blueprints and using them for a second theatre. You might have seen a twin of the Bloordale in another part of Toronto.

Archives of Ontario: RG56-11/ 6.50

Lansdowne (1942) *683 Lansdowne Ave., east side, north of Bloor St.*

It was built in the 1920s as the Park, then, in 1937, became the Lansdowne. In common with many early theatres, it was built to showcase live acts and musicals. Locals might remember the ubiquitous Ken Soble Amateur Hour, with Rudy Spratt and his orchestra, on stage in the 1940s. The theatre was managed for many years by Abe Polakoff, who was a member of the Lester family. As the marquee illustrates, you could see two features, a cartoon and the latest Joe Louis fight.

National Archives of Canada: MISA-4559-8

Beaver (1930) *2942 Dundas St. West, north side, near Pacific Ave.*

It was built in 1913, a very lavish movie house for the location. The Allens bought the theatre right after World War One, in one of their first invasions into the Toronto scene. The Beaver was unique in that it existed through to 1961 under its original name, although as a 20th Century theatre. As one of the first movie houses in the west end, it drew patrons from far and wide.

National Archives of Canada: PA: 11956

Runnymede (1927) 2225 Bloor St. West, south side, at Runnymede Rd.

The Capitol (Famous Players) group opened this wonderful theatre in June 1927. It was Toronto's first Atmospheric theatre, designed by Alfred Chapman, his only movie house. His fame came from work done on the Royal Ontario Museum. Also, he was father of the noted Toronto filmmaker, Chris Chapman. The "Runny" was a very popular, large, 1400-seat theatre that brought prestige to the west end of the city. It was billed as "Canada's Theatre Beautiful", with the best in music and popular stage shows. All this in the silent era! The Runnymede opened with an MGM popular comedy, 'The Rookies'. Although there was a fight to keep it as a theatre, in the late 1990s, the Runnymede became a Chapters bookstore.

U. of Calgary Archives: Pan. 61533-2K

Humber (1951) *2442 Bloor St. West, north side, west of Jane St.*

This is the only remaining example of a theatre built by J. Arthur Rank, whose Odeon chain appeared on the Toronto scene after World War Two. A large, lavish, first-run house when it opened, it is now a neighbourhood Cineplex multi-screen theatre. In 1946 the author helped build the Humber. Despite this, it has stood the test of time, having lasted over 50 years as a movie theatre, much longer than most of our "Nabes".

Apollo (1934) *2901 Dundas St.West, north side, in West Toronto Junction*

A typical storefront theatre of no particular architecture style, it had been around from the silent days as the Crystal, when the Blooms of B&F fame owned it. In the late 1930s, with a name change to the Apollo, it had to compete with the Mavety, the Beaver, the Crescent, the Prince James and the Wonderland theatres in the Junction. The Apollo's long narrow configuration was nicknamed a "shooting gallery" in the trade.

City of Toronto Archives: SC488-1105

Biltmore Weston (1953) *1831Weston Rd., east side, south of Lawrence Ave.*

By 1953, a new chain of theatres appeared around Toronto, the Biltmore Theatres. Even though this postwar movie house had been around for a few years as part of the National chain, it formed part of the Biltmore group, which became a driving force in the city. It was one of the first theatres to boast of its free parking.

Archives of Ontario: RG 56-11-0-349-3

Esquire (1939) *2290 Bloor St. West, north side, at Durie St.*

Situated in what is now the trendy Bloor West Village, it is too bad the venerable "Esky" could not have survived to see this. In the 1930s, the Esquire was one of the more important 20th Century theatres, cheek by jowl with the Royal Bank of Canada, and a Dominion store. It started life as the Lyndhurst, the name of the local telephone exchange. As a "subsequent" (third run) theatre, the Esquire survived for years in the shadow of the more important Runnymede, proving there was a place in the hierarchy of the movie house business for the little guy.

City of Toronto Archives: SC 488-1149

West End (1956) *215 Mavety St., east side, west of Keele and Dundas.*

Another of the name changers, the West End originally was named the Mavety for the street it was on. A long time member of the Allied chain, it was their presence in the Junction. This theatre was one of our earliest "Nabes", being built in 1921, eight years after the more important Beaver, just a block away. It may be a coincidence, but the main courier of films to theatres is called Mavety.

Toronto Reference Library.

Mayfair (1930) *347 Jane St., east side, below Annette St.*

This was the farthest west theatre in the city of Toronto when built in 1928. It soon upgraded to sound. The Mayfair also had aspirations to being an Atmospheric house, with a sailing ship motif. It was one of four or five movie houses built in a Toronto residential area.

City of Toronto Archives: SC.488-3200.

Weston (Fox) (1947) *2050 Weston Rd., west side, north of Lawrence Ave.*

The Weston, later the Fox Weston, was built and owned, in the 1920s, by the Scott family, and as Elwy Yost explained it was managed by Mr. Scott. It was then the Town of Weston's only movie house, and existed well into the 1950s despite stiff competition from the newer Biltmore, down the street. It was finally demolished to make way for a new government building and post office.

Archives of Ontario: RG 56-11-0-348-2

Kingsway (1976) *3030 Bloor St. West, north side, west of Royal York Rd.*

Another Art Deco theatre built in late 1939, just in time to start showing war films, it finally gave the Kingsway district and mid-Etobicoke its own theatre. Although south, in the more blue-collar New Toronto, the large 1100-seat Capitol had been in business for years. The Kingsway Theatre remains one of the few "Nabes" still in business, and was the first movie house in the current Festival chain. When first built, it had many modern design features, such as a glassed-in, soundproof, baby crying room in the balcony, so new mothers could bring their babies to the movies. It was owned and managed by Brock Farrow, whose family also owned the Vogue Theatre in Port Credit.

Photo: John Thompson

The Danforth

Bloor-Danforth, with 13 "Nabes" on the Danforth and a further 13 on Bloor Street, qualified as the biggest theatre street in Toronto. The Century, formerly the Allen Danforth, was the first grand movie house in the east end. The Prince Edward Viaduct almost made the Danforth into a separate city, and, as such, the locals supported their own theatres. There was no need to go over the bridge to a movie. Therefore, over the years, 13 movie houses sprouted up from Dawes Rd. to Broadview, on the Danforth and several north-south streets.

Cameo (1934) *989 Pape Ave., east side, near Cosburn Ave.*

Designed by Kaplan & Sprachman in 1934 for Sam and Bertha Strashin, it stayed in the Strashin family its entire life. It had all the earmarks of a mid 1930s movie house: apartment upstairs, box office in front, and a confectionery store built into the edifice. After a long, successful run, it was sold in the late 1950s to Loblaws. It is now a Canada Trust office, where you can still see vestiges of its Art Deco trim.

Strashin Family Archives.

Palace (1948) *664 Danforth Ave., north side, east of Pape Ave.*

This was Famous Players' large presence on the Danforth. A huge, 1500-seat theatre, it was built in 1921, and had the same legendary manager, Charlie Querrie, for over 25 years. Like many other prestige houses during the Depression, they kept 500 seats at a lower (25 cents) price. The Palace was so popular that it was one of the very few "Nabes" to run continuous shows, meaning you could go to a matinee during the week. This venerable old theatre, before being torn down, finished its days again as a movie theatre, after being faced with the ignominy of being reduced to a bingo parlour.

Granada (1937) *415 Danforth Ave., south side, at Logan Ave.*

Another typical "Nabe", this 500-seat house was built in the 1920s as the Model. It was independently owned under the Allied aegis after the war. For many years it was operated by Oscar Hanson, an important figure in the Toronto theatre scene. Because of its architecture, the Granada was easy to convert to a Greek restaurant, adding to the many in this area. As an important neighbourhood meeting place, the Model lent its name to many local businesses. In the 1950s, after the name change, recently-arrived locals wondered why a store across the street from the Granada was called the "Model Fish and Chip Shop".

Mandel Sprachman Archives.

Century (1940) *147 Danforth Ave., south side, east of Broadview Ave.*

This is one of Toronto's pioneer neighbourhood palaces. It was built as the Allen Danforth in 1919, a sister to the Tivoli and the Bloor. All were lavish, and designed by C.Howard Crane of Detroit. When hard times hit the Allen chain in 1923, most of their theatres were taken over by Famous Players. The Century ended up under B&F management and was the largest in their chain. It survives today as the Music Hall movie theatre, part of the Festival chain.

Archives of Ontario: RG 56-11/6.8

Donlands (1950) *397 Donlands Ave., east side, south of O'Connor Dr.*

Built around 1949 by the B&F group, the Donlands was one of the most modern "Nabes", architecturally speaking. Set in East York, it served the urban growth, new to this area. The building still stands, but shows no movies. It is a good example of postwar theatre architecture, which was quite distinctive when compared to the Art Deco theatres.

National Archives of Canada: PA-118945

Oxford (1938) *1512 Danforth Ave., north side, near Monarch Park Ave.*

Another old-fashioned, east end neighbourhood theatre, built in the old style with apartments above. It changed to B&F ownership in 1942, when Associated became 20th Century.

City of Toronto Archives: SC.488-1136.

Allenby (1936) *1215 Danforth , south side, east of Greenwood Ave.*

Independently owned at first, then part of the Allied Group. With 775 seats, it was large for a neighbourhood show. Architects Kaplan & Sprachman designed the theatre in 1936. When it opened it was a good example of the Art Deco period. The Allenby had a renewed lease on life in the 1960s when, with a name change to the Roxy, it became one of the city's first revival theatres, known as the "99-cent Roxy". Its success was widely imitated, and the building is still in business, operating as the Grand.

City of Toronto Archives: SC 488-1116

Community (1938) *1202 Woodbine Ave., west side, near Mortimer Ave.*

Built in the Art Deco style by Kaplan & Sprachman for B&F, its fate, along with the Carlton, was to close and become a TV film studio, in this case for Ralph Foster, an early pioneer in Canadian Film production.

City of Toronto Archives: SC.488-1142

Grover (1930) *2714 Danforth Ave., north side, at Dawes Rd.*

An early movie house from the 1920s, it joined the B&F Group in the 1930s, and, with several updates, lasted into the 1950s. It is now the Thunder nightclub. In its heyday, the Grover was one of Toronto's most easterly movie houses. It was another Toronto theatre named after a local telephone exchange.

City of Toronto Archives: SC488-2960.

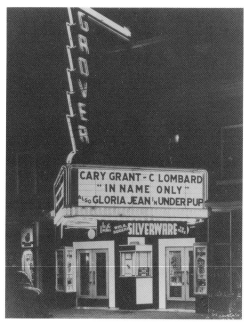

St. Clair Area

Some very old theatres shared this space with the most modern neighbourhood theatres: the Christie and the Royal George, with the Vaughan and Radio City. This strip was essentially a middle class neighbourhood, and the theatres reflected this.

Vaughan (1947) *558 St. Clair Ave. West, north side, at Vaughan Rd.*

In 1947, the B&F chain built a new, luxurious showplace on St. Clair called the Vaughan. It was to be their showpiece for the postwar years in the west end, having equal billing with the Century on the Danforth. With almost 1000 seats, it was even larger than their recently built Donlands in East York. The building was demolished in the 1980s, and there is not a trace of this grand show-place.

Archives of Ontario: RG 56-11-7.2

Royce (1930) *1619 Dupont St., south side, near the West Toronto Junction*

An old movie house built in the early 1920s, it capitalized on its proximity to the West Toronto stations, just a stone's throw away. The Royce spent its last years as one of the Allens' Premier theatres. Older Toronto residents will not be surprised by its name, as Dupont St. was known as Royce before the war.

City of Toronto Archives: SC.488-3500

Royal George (1954) *1217 St. Clair Ave. West, south side, west of Dufferin Street*

This theatre, another old timer, was built in 1919 on the then western end of St. Clair. The Royal George was a long time independent of 500 seats. It is interesting to note that, presumably because of the proximity to the First World War, our theatres' names reflected an obsession with Great Britain and Royalty. We see, besides the Royal George, names such as the Royal, Royal Alexandra, Palace, Regent, Empire, Avon, Strand, Prince of Wales, Prince Edward, Prince James, Monarch, Victoria, Queen, Queens Royal, King, Kings Playhouse, Crown, Rex, Regal and Brighton. Most of these went on to early name changes, but the Royal George kept its name till the 1960s, when it became the Continental. The building finally morphed into a very popular Italian specialty food store.

Photo: Harvey Naylor, Greenwood, N.S.

Colony (1939) *1801 Eglinton Ave. West, south side, east of Dufferin St.*

This prewar theatre was pretty much alone on the far west end of Eglinton Ave. for years. It had a hard time finding its niche, changing hands and distributors many times, until finally, in 1952, it was taken over and brought up to date by the Odeon chain, with which it finished its days. It bears a striking resemblance to the Metro theatre on Bloor Street. Like many other "Nabes", the building was torn down and replaced with an office building.

Mandel Sprachman Archives.

Grant (1937) *522 Oakwood Ave., west side, at Vaughan Rd.*

This typical "Nabe" had the look of a 1929 theatre, which actually was when it was built. It would look right at home on the main street of a small town. The Grant was independently owned and was quite popular in the 1930s, when you could get free parking with your 20-cent admission. After a renovation in 1937, it reopened as the New Grant, but subsequently reverted to its original name.

St. Clair (1950) *1154 St. Clair Ave. West, north side, east of Dufferin St.*

This theatre was built in 1921 as part of an eight-theatre incursion by the Allen group into Toronto. Its architect, F. Howard Crane of Detroit, used exactly the same design for the Beach and the Parkdale, - all large, 1400-seat theatres. His design was contrary to the normal practice of having the theatre entrance on the main street and the auditorium on less expensive property in the rear. These three theatres were built entirely on the main street, probably because of cheaper suburban real estate in 1920s Toronto. Historically, this has made it easier to convert these movie houses to boutiques and malls. In its last days as a movie theatre, it fell under the auspices of Lionel Lester, who converted it to a two screen house showing Italian films.

National Archives of Canada:

MISA-4564-22

Radio City (1942) *1454 Bathurst St., west side, south of St. Clair Ave. West*

A very important theatre built in the 1930s, it became a first run house of the Associated chain, along with the Madison. The Radio City joined the B&F chain in 1941. The theatre was built to stage live shows, and in later years that gave it a new lease on life. When the motion picture business declined, the Radio City became a popular venue to stage legitimate theatre, as well as persisting with movies.

Archives of Ontario: RG.56-11: 6.44.

An old fashioned theatre in the Famous Players chain, complete with crystal chandeliers, the Oakwood sat in an island surrounded by a streetcar loop. There must have been a lot of moviegoers in this area to fill its 1400 seats, as well as the 1450 seats at the nearby St. Clair Theatre. The Oakwood was demolished in the early 1960s and replaced with an apartment building.

Mandel Sprachman Archives

Oakwood (1940) 165 Oakwood Ave., east side, north of St. Clair Ave.

Major St. Clair (1945) *1780 St. Clair Ave. West, north side, east of Old Weston Rd.*

One of the few theatres left in the reborn Allen group, most of which were in the suburbs. The Allens had a lock on local moviegoers with fellow theatres close by, the Major Rogers Road, and the Major Mount Dennis. Like its "Nabes" to the south in the Junction, this was a working man's theatre. It was easily converted to a church.

Archives of Ontario: RG.56-11/6.1

JOHN BEAL IN G. STRATTON PORTER'S LADDIE
ALSO RICHARD DIX IN THE ARIZONIAN

SPECIAL MAT.
MON & WED 20-10

Paramount (1937) *1069 St. Clair Ave. West, south side, east of Dufferin St.*

It not only borrowed the name, but also the logo, of one of Hollywood's largest movie studios, while having no association with them. The Paramount had one of the city's more unusual promotions: the mind reader "Mystic Temple", who gave patrons private readings in the lobby. Later their promotions were more conventional, with "Rosy Bower" dinnerware as a giveaway.

Archives of Ontario: SC.488-4800.

College/Queen/Dundas West

This cluster of movie houses on College Street west of Spadina presents an interesting study group. The question arises how it was possible to have such a concentration of successful "Nabes" in such a small space. This is especially interesting, considering that, just to the north, on Bloor St. there were nine more, and south on Dundas and Queen another dozen. Most dated from the 1920s, but the last, the Pylon, was built in 1939 by one of the most knowledgeable people in the Canadian movie business. She was Ray Lewis, publisher of the Canadian Moving Picture Digest. Mrs. Lewis obviously thought that the area had the potential to support one more theatre. It was a working class district with a mostly Jewish population in the 1930s, but this changed later, giving way to Italian and Portuguese immigrants. The one thing they had in common was that their main entertainment was the movies, which made this concentration of theatres possible. These theatres were all small, mostly owner-managed. They were successful through the Depression, the Second World War, and the final years of neighbourhood movie going, with most lasting into the 1960s.

There were, apart from those mentioned, many more theatres in the early years. Queen West alone had the Photodrome, Maple Leaf, Reo, Peoples, Temple, Criterion, Paramount and Adanac.

Kum-C (1943) *1288 Queen St. West, north side, west of Dufferin St.*

One of those cleverly named movie houses, a holdover from the silent days. It was the rerun theatre for the Parkdale area. As part of Nat Taylor's 20th Century chain, the Kum-C lasted well into the 1960s. In its last days it became popular again, with a revival policy of three or four features a day for $1.00.

Archives of Ontario: RG.56-11/6.28

Bellevue (1938) *360 College St., north side, east of Bathurst St.*

B&F built this large theatre of 800 seats in the depth of the Depression as the Shaw. It was one of a cluster of movie houses in the College/Bathurst area, and shows the familiar earmarks of one of Kaplan & Sprachman's Art Deco designs. A name change to the Electra to attract the ethnic market failed, and the theatre ended its days as Toronto's last burlesque house, the Lux.

Mandel Sprachman Archives

The name Pylon sounds strange today, but in 1939, when it was built, a pylon was a popular signaling device used at airports and in air races. The theatre's slogan was "We are a beacon for good entertainment". It's not surprising that the present owners changed the name to the Royal. A very influential woman, Ray Lewis, who published 'The Canadian Moving Picture Digest', built the theatre. It was designed by Ben Swartz, whose design included, in the back of the building, a dance hall and roller skating rink. Lewis knew everyone in the trade, from moguls to movie stars. Her friend Anna Neagle, a top British star, was visiting Toronto to publicize her film, 'Nurse Edith Cavell', and left her footprints in the newly poured concrete floor in the lobby. They remain there, under the carpet, today.

York University Archives: 1974-COZ- G-11 (246)

College (1940) *960 College St., northwest corner of Dovercourt Rd.*

Although built in 1921 by the Allens, this theatre spent its whole life as a Famous Players theatre. Large, with 1500 seats, it was the biggest of the eight movie houses on that stretch of College Street. The College almost went under in 1935 at the height of the Depression, but staged a spectacular comeback during the war years due to the influx of workers from nearby west end war plants

National Archives of Canada:

PA111080

Brock (1942) *1585 Dundas St. West, south side, at Brock Ave.*

As the early Dundas Theatre, built in the silent years, this theatre was redone in 1935 by Kaplan & Sprachman with an Art Deco décor. Of particular interest is the perfect out-front box office with porthole. The marquee is very similar to the architects' Grant Theatre.

National Archives of Canada: PA-111032

Playhouse (Melody) (1937) *344 College St., north side, near Brunswick Ave.*

This was strictly a neighbourhood show, and, like many in the same boat, they didn't bother to advertise, figuring the locals would walk by and notice what was playing. After years under this name, it became the Melody, and for a while the All Nations. The theatre had been at this location for many years when the much larger and more modern B&F Bellevue moved in almost next door. This was a fate that happened to many "Nabes" when they became too successful.

City of Toronto Archives: SC.488-1099

Pix (Aster) (1942) *233 Ossington Ave., east side, south of Dundas St.*

This neat little theatre (450 seats), one of the smallest in the city, started life as the Aster, when it was fashionable to name theatres after birds and flowers. The architecture, with its Greek Revival columns, tended to make it look like a bank; this was prophetic, as the theatre ended up as a CIBC bank. This was after a name change to the Pix, postwar.

National Archives of Canada: Pa 111167.

Parkdale (1937) *1605 Queen St. West, south side, east of Roncesvalles Ave.*

This was one of eight Toronto theatres, built by the Allens in the early 1920s, that were designed by C. Howard Crane. It bore an uncanny resemblance to another of his designs, the St. Clair. The Parkdale became a Famous Players house after the Allen business setback in 1923. With its location right above the popular Sunnyside Amusement Park, the theatre profited from the crowds escaping the city.

Archives of Ontario: RG.56-11/6.43

Studio (King) (1974) *565 College St., south side, at Manning Ave.*

George A. Lester's second theatre, built after the Royal across the street, was a very popular neighbourhood house. Lester himself was an institution on College St. In the 1950s, when movie going ran out of steam, sons Lionel and Robert took control. They changed the name to the Studio and brought in Italian pictures for the new inhabitants in the neighbourhood. The theatre in turn became a popular art house.

York University Archives: 1974-002/246

Orpheum (1977) *600 Queen St. West, north side, west of Bathurst Street*

All but unknown to any but the locals, this Queen and Bathurst theatre, like most of the Queen St. West theatres, never advertised. The Orpheum outlasted its neighbour, the tiny Chateau, only a block to the east, by almost 20 years, closing in the 1970s. It was said to have had a unique auditorium configuration, with a reverse sloping floor, which meant its floor sloped upward, unlike the usual downward slope. The building remains, very much as in its heyday, with the marquee still in use.

Photo: John Thompson.

Centre (1945) *772 Dundas St. West, north side, west of Bathurst St.*

It gained notoriety as the Duchess Theatre in 1933, when its owner was arrested for hiring two thugs to beat up a neighbouring theatre owner. Shortly after came the name change, which was certainly accurate, as it was close to the centre of Toronto.

Archives of Ontario: RG 56-11/6.

This venerable old theatre dates back to 1908 when it opened as the Auditorium, showing early films. in 1913 it became the Avenue, soon changed in 1915 to salute America's sweetheart, Mary Pickford, born not far from the theatre. Shortened to the Pickford, it kept that name until 1945, when it became the Variety. Housed in an historic Toronto building, the Variety was closed in the 1950s and the building finally demolished to make way for a fast food restaurant.

Pickford (1956) *382 Queen Street West, northwest corner of Spadina Ave.*

There were a few "Nabes" spotted along Bloor west of Bathurst in the earliest years. The Paradise, (then known as the Kitchener), the Academy, and the Doric. These theatres all did well. Bathurst and Bloor, by 1920, was considered the main intersection of mid Toronto. The splendid Madison on Bloor was built first. The Allens then put in their Bloor across the street. Famous Players, not to be outdone, opened the Alhambra. Thus, there were three major movie houses within two blocks, representing the three major circuits.

Alhambra (1950) *568 Bloor St. West, north side, west of Bathurst St.*

A large, luxurious house with 1000 seats, it was one of the first Famous Players theatres. When Famous Players took over the Bloor from the Allens, it, incongruously, left the Bathurst and Bloor intersection with two Famous Players theatres out of three major movie houses. Before being renovated, it was one of the city's best-looking classic theatres and a favourite with the locals. One former usher remembers an extra perk in that they had reciprocating freebies with the neighbouring Midtown.

U of Calgary Archives: Pan-49874-5

Midtown (Madison) (1942) *506 Bloor St. West, north side, east of Bathurst St.*

This 20th Century theatre had to be good to compete with its neighbours, Famous Players' luxurious Bloor and Alhambra Theatres. It was a large, 1100-seat, sometimes first run house, with a history. As the Madison, it advertised itself as "Midcity's Popular Theatre". It had a two-tier pricing structure: the centre portion of the house was 35 cents, and the side sections, 25 cents. In 1940, with the theatre showing its age, there was a complete renovation and modernization, which included the first twin (love) seats in a theatre in Toronto. The name was changed to the Midtown, and for a time it was one of Toronto's swankiest theatres. Today, with the adopted name of its neighbour, the former Madison

does business as the Bloor, but its most popular days were as the Midtown, and it was also known at various times as the Capri and the Eden.

City of Toronto Archives: SC488-6047—Madison: RG 8-S7-161

Adelphi (1936) *1008 Dovercourt Rd., west side, north of Bloor St.*

This theatre started life as the Cum-Bac, an independent. Its owner, a Mr. Bailie, became President of the Allied Theatres chain in 1936. The Adelphi was unusual in that it was located on a north/south street in a residential area. The Adelphi, in common with a few of our movie houses, has become a church.

City of Toronto Archives: SC488-1108

Updated in 1935, this silent era movie house followed Nat Taylor into the 20th Century chain in 1942. It stayed there until the end of its days. Like many theatres, it shared its exterior with a cigar store. In the early days, the Kenwood had the Regal as a neighbour and later, just a few doors away, the Metro, the Doric and the Paradise. In the golden days, they all prospered.

National Archives of Canada: PA 111143

Kenwood (1942) 962 Bloor St. West, north side, near Dovercourt Rd.

Academy (1938) *1286 Bloor Street W., north side, near Lansdowne Ave.*

A small independent sandwiched between the larger Lansdowne and Kenwood. It held its own with a fare of action movies. A storefront theatre, like many, the Academy had a pool hall upstairs.

Today, the building remains almost the same as when movies were shown there, changing hands and purpose almost yearly.

Archives of Ontario: RG 56-11/ 5.46

There has been a theatre on this sight since the early teens; the first was the Bloor Palace. After World War One, it was changed to the Kitchener—a tip of the hat to the British Field Marshall, Lord Kitchener, a hero of The Great War. In 1939, after a redo, by Kaplan & Sprachman, the theatre acquired its Art Deco façade and new name, the New Paradise. This was later shortened to the Paradise, as it is known today. The building is now part of a small chain of six surviving neighbourhood theatres.

Archives of Ontario: RG 56-11/6.41

Paradise (1948) *1008 Bloor St. West, north side, west of Ossington Ave.*

Metro (1950) *679 Bloor St. West, south side, at Manning Ave.*

Built in 1938, it was one of the last Art Deco theatres built by Kaplan & Sprachman, before the war. The Metro has survived as a multi-screen art house, with a slant towards erotic pictures. It is the sole survivor of a group of five theatres in this area, lasting only because the owner had the foresight to buy up rights to some features that became available. The Metro started life with a bang when it had the misfortune to have a massive fire on opening night. The ensuing picture coverage in all the local newspapers gave operator Manny Stein a lot of unexpected publicity.

Mandel Sprachman Archives.

Almost Survivors

This is a group of "Nabes", scattered around Toronto, that we haven't been able to locate original photos of, but were important theatres in their day. All the buildings, once theatres, still exist today, 2001. The Avon, originally the grand King's Playhouse, is now a display sign studio. The Bloor, once a fine Famous Players showplace, is now Lee's Palace, a rock concert hall. The Brighton, still sporting its marquee, is now a convenience store. The recycled Classic theatre is a second-hand store. The Garden and Vogue look like they could start showing movies tomorrow. Uniquely, the Bonita is still a movie house, but name changed to the Wellington. The Ace on the Danforth, started life as the Iola, was briefly the Regal, then assumed the name and marquee of the old Ace on Queen at Bay. It is now a drug store.

Classic *1300 Gerrard St. E.*

Avon *1092 Queen St. W.*

Bloor *529 Bloor St. W.*

Garden *290 College St.*

Ace *603 Danforth Ave.*

Vogue *1574 Queen St. E.*

Brighton *127 Roncesvalles Ave.*

Bonita *1035 Gerrard St. E.*

Reminiscences

"Hey, do you remember the old..."

Norman Jewison, filmmaker

I remember when I was very young and growing up in the Beaches area of Toronto, I had a hand-cranked movie projector and would show movies in our basement. Then when I was seven or eight I started going to movie theatres. The first one was the Beach on Queen. I used to go to Saturday matinees, where for 10 cents you could see a newsreel, a cartoon, a short comedy, a serial and two features, so you were in the theatre from two o'clock until five-thirty. But the one I remember most was the Family, again on Queen, at Lee. I think they later changed the name to the Lake. What I remember was that it was downstairs from a pool hall, and every time there was a dramatic silent pause in the movie you would hear the click, click, click of the billiard balls. It sure killed the drama. The first money I made from the movies was during the Depression. No one had any money so, after seeing a film, I would *tell* the movie to a group of kids, and they would give me a penny.

David Crombie, former Mayor of Toronto

I learned a lot about life at the Runnymede Theatre. Like all kids, my brother and I looked forward every Saturday to the afternoon matinee. We were able to join our pals and immerse ourselves in the weekly fare of two movies, a cartoon, a serial, " News of the Day", selected shorts, and previews. For 12 cents a ticket, it was an unbelievable cornucopia of entertainment.

But we had newspapers to do. We delivered both morning and evening papers (Globes, Stars and Telys), and maintained an outlet at the corner of Jane and Bloor, where the Bloor streetcars used to turn. On Saturdays, we had to fit the "show" in between our Globe route, followed by Saturday morning collections and picking up the home edition for the corner sale in the afternoon. Timing and discipline became paramount.

In practical terms this meant we couldn't see all of the afternoon show unless one or the other of us was willing to shoulder the extra responsibility. In short, we had to balance our pleasures with our obligations and trust one another. In doing so, we earned a special benefit. From time to time, Mum allowed us to go to the early evening show as a reward for what we had to miss.

Those evening shows at the Runnymede were the sweetest of all.

Robert Fulford, writer

In the 1940s the Beach district was splendidly supplied with movie theatres, five in all, including the Fox (still breathing today) and the grander (but now deceased) Beach Theatre, which was so classy that the Saturday matinee cost 25 cents and the manager never failed to wear a tux. But my heart belongs to the Manor. It was a movie house like no other, on Kingston Road near Silver Birch Ave. In retrospect it seems poignantly tiny, a dinghy up against yachts. It announced itself with a marquee you couldn't see from a block away, with a two-feet-high letterboard giving the name of whatever wretched old movie was playing. It was smelly, but the price was right. We got in for 12 cents on most Saturday afternoons, and there were occasions (loss-leader days, I imagine) when six cents did the trick. The movies were always simple-minded and boyish, which made them perfect: there was no danger of encountering a plot about kissing and stuff. These were "C" pictures, frequently Westerns pumped out by Republic in its dark, soupy, not-quite-colour technique; watching them was like looking at the world through a brown sweater. But audience participation brought the Manor to life. Let me put it this way: it was *mandatory* to fire your cap gun at the screen when Hopalong Cassidy fought the bad guys, as he did just about every Saturday of my childhood, and it was unpatriotic *not* to hiss Japanese fighter pilots as soon as they appeared. When not pursuing these activities, we chased each other up and down the aisles. We thought it was fun. Fifty years later we learned it was Attention Deficit Disorder.

Gary Ross, editor
From Cottingham Street, where I grew up, the quickest way to the Vaughan Theatre was also the diciest—through the ravine that runs from Boulton Avenue past the Winston Churchill Reservoir and under Spadina Road, emerging at St. Clair near Bathurst. This was the ravine in which I learned what a condom was, and where I first tasted gin. One Saturday afternoon, the summer I was 11, I became the victim of armed robbery.

Two teenagers materialized on the opposite side of the creek that used to bisect the ravine. I walked faster. They walked faster. I broke into a trot. They began running.

When they crossed the bridge ahead of me, cutting me off, I knew I was in trouble. One kid had a kitchen knife and held the point under my chin, like they do in gangster movies. I rummaged in my pockets as if looking for money. Then I reached for the sky, like they do in cowboy movies. The other kid searched me and came up with thirty-five cents. "That's all?" "That's all," I said, then took off, running as fast as I could, not only because I was scared but because I was afraid I'd be late for the matinee. I emerged onto St. Clair West panting and trembling, crossed the street, and hurried toward the box office, the crumpled dollar bill clutched in my right hand.

Al Waxman, actor
Deceased/January 2001,
as told to Ed Cowan/October 2000.
There were so many movie houses in the Spadina/Dundas/College Street area, such as the La Salle and the Garden, but I remember with real joy those important Saturdays when Al "Duke" (now Federal Judge Alan) Linden and I would go to the Victory Theatre at the corner of Spadina and Dundas. Later it would become a strip theatre and a Chinese cinema. Back in the late, late 1940s and early 1950s, with the 25 cents allowance we were given by our parents, we would feast ourselves on a hot dog and a Coke at Shopsy's, the delicatessen's original Spadina location right beside the theatre, and have enough money left over for the matinee. Needless to say, most Saturdays we walked to the theatre and home.

Beverly Rockett Roberts, photographer
It was really those Saturday afternoon matinees at the Esquire. I cannot forget the constant din of all the kids screaming at once (like they do at a Michael Jackson con-

cert). It was bedlam. Those "dirty/nasty" little boys… wrestling in the aisles…on and over the seats…all around you. All of this, of course, was pure early male bravado, rough house to impress, sexual posturing, if you like, and the girls just loved it…and they screamed with delight. My "Nabe" territory included the Esquire, the Kingsway and the Runnymede. I was very lucky, because my parents were movie junkies, went twice a week, midweek when the features changed. They would take me along (my dad was mad for Maureen O'Hara and Paulette Goddard). So sometimes, I would get to go to the movies three times in one week. The choice of theatre for the Saturday matinee was usually a question of economics. The tickets at the Esquire were usually five cents while the larger and more garishly stylish Runnymede was 10 cents. Besides, if I and my movie companion Joey (a girl, of course) chose the Esquire we could always, on the way to the theatre, "check out the action at the Kresges and Woolworths Five and Dime stores", the Holt Renfrew of our under 10 set.

Mike Filey, writer/historian

One of the great things about growing up in Toronto was the remarkable profusion of movie theatres scattered all over town. Downtown were the large movie houses, places like the cavernous Shea's Hippodrome on Bay, Loew's (now Elgin), Imperial (now Pantages), Uptown on Yonge, and the Tivoli on Richmond at Victoria.

For me, visits to these theatres were infrequent, and usually only happened when taken to one of them by my parents. On the other hand, a visit to one of my neighbourhood theatres was much easier to pull off. And boy, did I have a bunch to choose from. I was fortunate to grow up near the busy Bloor and Bathurst intersection. Nearby were four of the most exciting movie houses in the entire city. East of Bathurst were the Midtown and Bloor. Both structures are still there, the former a theatre now renamed the Bloor and the latter occupied by a restaurant. A few doors west of the intersection was the Alhambra, now the site of a Swiss Chalet restaurant, while even further west the little Metro, which at last visit was still there.

Over the years I visited all four on numerous occasions, but it's safe to say that my favourite was, without doubt, the Alhambra. That was probably because of something that happened in 1949. One afternoon I became so captivated by 'The Wizard of Oz' that I sat through several showings, eventually being forcibly retrieved from my trance by my somewhat agitated father. And I'll never forget Pat Tobin, the theatre manager, who was more than partially responsible for my allegiance to the Alhambra. Each Sunday he'd invite me to come to the theatre and help clean the place. With no Sunday showings back then, I had the place to myself. And so what if I didn't get paid. I had all the day-old popcorn I could ever want.

Jack Batten, writer

The theory my group came up with, when we were all 11 years old, was that a kid wasn't allowed into a movie theatre if, by the time the movie ended, it was dark outside. That, we figured, was the rule in the adult world. This was why all of us had to go to the Saturday matinees at one in the afternoon.

However, on a November Saturday in 1942, I put the rule to the test at the Avenue Theatre. The Avenue was one of my locals, a small, tidily laid out theatre a short bike ride from my house. On this particular Saturday, for reasons I've forgotten, I couldn't make the one o'clock matinee. I went at four. The movie was 'Gentleman Jim', starring Errol Flynn as Jim Corbett, the heavyweight boxing champ. I wondered if the woman in the box office would sell me a ticket. She did, a regular 12-cent kids' ticket. I sat in an aisle seat close to the front. I was cautiously elated. Maybe I've cheated the adults system.

Then terror struck. The usher, a woman about 20, shone her flashlight into my face. "You're not supposed to be in here," she said. Tears instantly filled my eyes. "But I couldn't come at one," I said, almost bawling. There was a long pause from the usher. "Okay," she said at last. "But don't cause trouble." Trouble? What trouble?

I sat through the movie, barely daring to breath. I watched 'Gentleman Jim', not entirely understanding the story. But I felt triumphant. I'd gone to the Avenue at four, and I'd beat the system.

Erna Paris, author

The old Village Theatre was on Spadina Road north of Lonsdale, on the west side of the street, and in the early 1950s it was a magical place. The promise of that darkened space before the projector was turned on, the excitement of seeing your school friends there – the girls crammed together with the girls, looking and whispering; the boys elbowing each other, and all of us squirming with expectation.

The Village reserved one night a week, I think it was Thursday, for what it called its "sneak preview." We never knew what we were going to see, which added to the suspense, but no one's parents needed to worry, since sex and extreme violence hadn't yet made their way to the public screen. In fact, I have *no* memory of the films we "previewed" at the Village, and I rather suspect they were the "B" (or was it the "Z"?) products of their day— the cheapest the management could procure. But whatever reel was rolling wasn't the point. What mattered was being there with the gang. What mattered was that our parents had let us come, and that (thank goodness) they weren't there with us.

I always think about the "sneaks" when I drive down Spadina Road, and the last time I looked there was a fast-food restaurant on the spot. So what, I say to myself in consolation, restaurants come and go. *I* know that for me and hundreds of other erstwhile "kids" from that distant era, they'll never erase the Village, where we stepped into the outside world for the very first time.

Charles Pachter, artist

In the early Fifties my uncle, Dave Kofsky, was a projectionist at the Beaver Theatre in The Junction, on Dundas west of Keele. During the matinee, I used to visit him up in the booth at the top of the second balcony. For a nine year old, it was a long climb up the steep steps, cluttered with popcorn and sticky Eskimo pie wrappers. When I finally made it, I would find him working away in his booth just under the roof. I watched with fascination as he rewound huge spools of 35mm film, which he would then stack in round shiny tin containers bigger than pie plates. I would squint through the glass projector window at Victor Mature and Debra Paget in gladiator togs and toga, locked in a suffocatingly tight clinch.

My neighbourhood theatre where I went most Saturdays was the Nortown, on Eglinton just west of Bathurst, only a block from our house. It's gone now, replaced by a featureless mini-mall. When I went to the Nortown it seemed glamorous, with shiny black Art Deco tiles and twinkling lights, though it wasn't as grand as the Eglinton a few blocks east. That was a real Art Deco palace, with alabaster sculptures of bare-naked ladies over the emergency exit doors.

At the Nortown I came second in the annual yo-yo contest. I also sat frozen with fear, mesmerized by Vincent Price in the 3-D horror movie 'House of Wax', and emerged ashen and trembling out of the dark theatre into the bright afternoon sunlight. In the Fifties, the movies still had more power to astonish and delight than anything on crude black and white TV.

PS. The Pickford is where my father worked as an usher in the 1930s. According to him, it was at the northwest corner of Queen and Spadina, where the McDonald's is now.

Adele Green, producer

The Palace, at Pape and Danforth, was my favourite "Nabe". I frequented the Century, the Cameo and the Granada but my heart belonged to the elegant Palace. I could depend on seeing one of the blondes; June Haver, Betty Grable or Doris Day, singing and dancing their way through yet another MGM musical. Of course, when I got home, I would sit in front of the mirror and do the routines all over again. Yes, I did have to sit through all the westerns, serials and cartoons that came before the main feature, but it was worth the wait. I also had to put up with all the little boys making airplanes out of their popcorn boxes and flying them up to the beautiful chandelier that hung in the Palace. In later years, it came as a great shock to find out that life isn't exactly like the movies; blondes come out of a bottle and we don't really live happily ever after. With one exception, me, I married the author.

Paul Break, writer

I grew up in The Beaches, from age five (1932), until I moved downtown in1954, with five neighbourhood movie houses: the Kingswood (a.k.a. the Manor) and the Scarboro, on Kingston Road, and the Beach, the Family, and the Fox (which we called the Morgue) on Queen Street East. I saw my first movie ever at the Kingswood: Laurel & Hardy in 'March of the Wooden Soldiers'; loved the weekly serials at the Scarboro; played pool overtop the Family; and lived through my teen angst at the Beach Theatre; but my heart belonged—and belongs—to the Fox.

I first went to the Fox in June of 1940, a 90-second sprint downhill from our house at 204 Beech Ave. Today, we drive out on warm Spring through Fall evenings, because The Beaches is a bitch on dark winter nights, and parking increasingly hard to find. The Kingswood, Scarboro and Family are long gone; the Beach name has been given a miraculous second coming as a multi-mini-movie palace farther west on Queen; but the old (Morgue) Fox rolls on, hopefully forever. And when the house lights dim, the boring everyday world of fantasy and illusion is replaced by the real world of drama, intrigue, love, laughter and happy endings, just like when I was a kid.

John Robert Colombo, writer

The library is my haunt, not the movie theatre.

For this reason, whenever I think of a particular movie theatre, I remember an outstanding feature film or short feature that I first saw on its screen. If I loved the film, I loved the theatre, whether grandiose or decrepit.

It is sad that the favourite neighbourhood theatres of my past are long gone. Question: *Where, oh where, are the movie houses of yesteryear?* Answer: They have been supplanted by Cineplexes and multiplexes with names like Silver City; may these like the Cities Service gas stations of old soon depart!

Here are some vignettes from my movie-going past.

As a student, I made my way from the campus of the University of Toronto (the centre of my world at the time) to the Radio City (Bathurst and St. Clair, the northern reaches of my Toronto in the 1950s) to watch the unforgettable 'Dr. Mabuse—The Gambler' and 'Dr. Mabuse—King of Crime', Fritz Lang's two-part silent productions starring Rudolf Klein-Rogge as the master criminal who so stunningly prefigured the approaching Nazi menace.

At the Uptown (Bloor St. at Yonge), I recall being overpowered by the colours and shapes of 'The Enchanted Owl', the NFB's short tribute to Eskimo printmaker Kenoujak. I seem to recall that it was also at the Uptown that I first saw, and heard, the most moving and intense short films ever released in this country: Norman McLaren's astonishing trilogy 'Pas de Deux', 'Ballet Adagio', and 'Narcissus'.

My wife Ruth and I experienced the Toronto premiere of '2001: A Space Odyssey' on the wide curved screen of the Glendale (Avenue Road north of Lawrence). Our companions were cineaste Elwy and Lila Yost, and that evening we spent hours puzzling about the "meaning" of the movie's "monolith."

Then there was the Christie (St. Clair Ave. West), which was owned by Bennett Fode, a native of Copenhagen. In Paris, he met Francois Truffaut, the director, who was then at the height of his fame. Fode boasted that he had convinced Truffaut to hold the North American premiere of his next nouvelle vague feature at the modest Christie. This never happened, of course.

If you feel my choice of cinemas is eccentric, you can imagine my choice of libraries!

Ed Cowan, media consultant
Thank God, it was very dark in the Circle that afternoon. The guys were four rows back and couldn't really see that I actually had gotten my arm around the back of the seat where, next to me, sat the "older girl", the fabulous 13-year old Jean Ferguson. Next, my hand dropped, ever so gently, to her far shoulder. The excitement was excruciating. She did not move. My hand stayed on that shoulder until Hopalong Cassidy, the cartoons and Pathe News were over and I had won the bet. The guys had to pay for my ticket that day. Those were the great days of the Saturday afternoon matinees at my "Nabes", the Circle and the Capital on Yonge St. north of Eglinton, and my "local", the Avenue at the top of my own street, Braemar Avenue. For years the Avenue was the centre of my weekly social life (especially when my older brother was head usher and I got "slipped in the back way"). I also used to improve my spelling by helping him change the marquee every week. Many "Nabes" also had full stages, and later in life the Avenue played host to Spring Thaw, and my first ever "live" play, "A View from the Bridge", starring the great American actor, Luther Adler. But my heart and mind will forever be there on that amazing afternoon with the fabulous Jean.

Don Shebib, filmmaker
The Ideal was my neighbourhood theatre, growing up in east end Toronto in the 1940s and 1950s. It was located on the west side of Main just south of Danforth, and every Saturday afternoon it became the centre of our world. It was small and intimate, long and narrow, resembling a bowling alley more than a movie theatre, but the time my friends and I spent there was magical. The films were the usual fare, cartoons, a serial and the feature was usually a comedy (Bowery Boys or Abbott and Costello), a Western (Roy, Gene or Hoppy) and, as we were still in the wake of World War Two, often a war film (John Wayne, of course). One of the great things about the experience was not only the enjoyment of the film, but the pleasure of acting out that film, and its usually

simplistic view of the world and its conflicts, during our play times for the next week, until the coming Saturday, when we would be launched again on another adventure. And unlike today, when we are bombarded with constant TV experiences, this once a week visual treat was looked on with great anticipation. Also, unlike today, the matinee experience was for kids only; there were seldom any adults present. Either you were old enough to go to the show by yourself, or you simply didn't go. The same was true for our sports. Parents never came to hockey or baseball games, even in the organized city leagues. This was a world for kids alone.

I was fortunate enough to be young in a time removed from the harm of World War Two, and spared the trauma of the turbulent Sixties and Vietnam, with only the rumblings of Rock 'n Roll to rustle the fabric of Eisenhower's America. True, there was a falseness to the conformity of it all, but we were too young to be concerned about that. Television brought an end to the matinees in the late Fifties, their time never to return again, and I am saddened that my own children were never able to partake of this great experience and the weekly anticipation of the new and exciting adventures that awaited us on each successive Saturday.

The Ideal closed down in the Sixties, and was turned into an apartment house, until, a few years ago, it was gutted by fire. Its shell still remains, half-hidden from view by the large bridge on Main Street that crosses the CNR tracks, just below the Danforth. Every time I pass by it, all those childhood memories come flooding back to me, all the films, and the adventures they inspired in my friends and I.

Harry Rasky, writer/filmmaker
The Royal George movie house on St.Clair was my escape. I danced with Fred Astaire. I dared with Paul

Muni. I memorized that speech in 'Emile Zola', defending Dreyfus, and I was Dreyfus, too. And do you remember when Muni and I discovered Pasturization? And Edward G. turned good guy to wipe out the plague or something in 'Magic Bullet'? We did that together. But it was okay because even then it was rumoured he was really a Jew posing as a gangster—he had a Jewish heart.

Glen Woodcock, editor/broadcaster
I can't remember exactly where it happened, at the Paradise or at the Doric, but I do know it was 1949 when I fell in love with an older woman.

The movie was 'Miracle on 34th Street', made two years earlier in 1947. Natalie Wood was nine. I was six. It was a one sided affair that lasted until her untimely death in 1981.

The Paradise and the Doric are interchangeable in my memory. Mere blocks apart on the north side of Bloor, just east of Dufferin Street, they were the neighbourhood theatres of my boyhood. It didn't seem to matter which one we went to; that all depended on the double bills playing on their screens that week. (Meaning, whichever was showing a Roy Rogers or Gene Autry movie, if I had any say in it. My sister held out for Esther Williams.)

Saturday matinees were for other kids. Friday night was our family's time at the movies until Dad brought home our first TV, a horribly unreliable Emerson, in 1953.

No matter which theatre we went to, my mother always picked the same place to sit: halfway down the right-hand aisle and then next to the wall. The four of us— my mother, my dad, my sister and me—probably occupied the entire short row. It's a habit I adopted, and retain to this day.

I remember very few of the titles we saw on their smallish screens—mostly war movies such as 'An American Guerilla in the Philippines', 'They Were Not Divided', and

'Flying Leathernecks'. What impressed my young mind more than the second-run B movies were the Popeye cartoons and the trailers. I still love trailers. And, of course, we all sang along as we followed the bouncing ball.

One other habit from those days has survived. Whenever things get repetitious I still say, "This is where we came in," just like Mom used to. No one too young to remember continuous showings at the neighbourhood theatre has any idea of what I'm talking about.

Mandel Sprachman, architect

My grandfather's house was a couple of blocks away from the Strand. Every Saturday afternoon I was disposed of there, with strict instructions to wait at grandfather's after the show for my parents. My father's firm, Kaplan & Sprachman Architects, renovated the Strand, and it became the Victory. I was an usher working in the balcony. 'The Great Waltz' played so long that I knew the lines by heart. The Russian films 'Quiet Flows the Don' and 'The Volga Boatman' (the Russians were our allies then) played just as long as 'The Great Waltz', however I never did learn any Russian. Later, as an architect, I renovated the Victory and it became the Golden Harvest. Of all my theatre work, the Golden Harvest was the most intriguing, because the theatre began catering to the Yiddish New Canadians and, with a few bumps in between, ended up catering to the Chinese New Canadians.

Vernon Chapman, actor

I once developed an affection for a movie house. In the mid-1930s, when I was 15, we moved to the suburb of Mimico. There were only two cinemas in the area, the Capitol in New Toronto, and the Rex in Mimico. To a teenager who aspired to be an actor, the picture house not only supplied entertainment, but became the classroom to study acting. Despite its name, the Rex was quite "un-kingly", but I preferred it to the Capitol, because it was closer, cosier and cheaper. I became a regular there, and in the later years of the Depression, for a mere 25 cents, I not only watched my favourite movie stars and picked up a lot about acting, but I could also pick up a different piece of gaudily ugly dinnerware each week. This I did until we had a complete set, which was worthy only of the kitchen. I inherited the set from my parents, and, in turn, unloaded it on my niece as a starter set when she got married. So, as a result of my constant patronage at the Rex, not only was I entertained and enlightened but also obtained tableware that has served at least two generations. In the postwar, post-dinnerware period, a friend of mine became the manager, and often let me in for free, which made visiting the Rex even more enjoyable. But soon, my beloved Rex succumbed to the onslaught of TV, and metamorphosed into a restaurant and cleaning emporium. Boo Hoo!

David Lewis Stein, writer

The Kent Theatre was on the west side of Yonge St., about half a block north of St. Clair Ave. Compared to the Hollywood, which was across the street and a little to the north, the Kent was small and dowdy, even in the early 1940s. However, the Kent charged only 12 cents for children, and we could spend all Saturday afternoon. There was one feature, then two or three cartoons, then previews of coming movies. These seemed to go on forever, because there were previews for the movies that would run on Monday, Tuesday and Wednesday, then for Thursday, Friday and Saturday. Then there was the news, when we went out to the washroom or wrestled in our seats unless there was something in the news about the war.

There would be an episode from a serial that we cheered for, then a second feature that always seemed to have many of the same actors as the first movie. My parents operated a cigar store lunch counter four blocks below St. Clair, at the corner of Yonge and Walker. They could not take me to the movies themselves on Saturday afternoons, so they hired a boy from the neighbourhood, Dave, to take me and a whole gang of kids from Walker and Alcorn up to the Kent. Dave was probably 14 or 15 but to the six and seven years olds he was shepherding up to the Kent every Saturday, he seemed like a "big kid". We got to be such fixtures that Dave was offered a position as assistant manager. My father said scornfully that his job was to fold up the seats and sweep the floor, but Dave went on to a whole career in the theatre business.

Years later, in the early Sixties, when I began courting my wife, Alison, I took her to the Kent. We saw 'The Grapes of Wrath'. My old neighbourhood movie had become an art theatre, just before it disappeared forever.

Bruce Gray, actor

When I was a teenager living in Toronto, the holiest site in my universe was not St.Peters. Nor Mecca. Nor Jerusalem. It was the Runnymede Theatre. That was where magic happened. And mystery. That was also where one learned important life lessons: how to tell good from bad, right from wrong. That was where you learned what it took to be a hero. And how to deal with adversity. "If at first you don't succeed…pick yourself up, dust yourself off, and start all over again."

The Runnymede was also where I learned that there is "No Business Like Show Business," and that "The Show must Go On." These are aphorisms that I still religiously adhere to even today. Did my acting career have its beginnings sitting there in the dark watching Betty Grable triumph against all adversity, save the show, trump the villain and live happily ever after with a succession of adoring leading men? We all wanted to be Betty.

From the age of 13 to 17, I firmly believed that Betty Grable was the greatest actress that ever lived. For one thing, she spoke English, which I found absolutely riveting. I had been brought up in Puerto Rico and my previous movie experiences were watching a lot of musta-chioed Latin Lotharios smooch their way into the arms of sultry babes with flashing eyes. And this being San Juan in the 1940s, they all spoke Spanish.

When I went to a special screening of 'Bambi', I was amazed to discover that Bambi and Thumper and Flower spoke in English. But I reasoned that animals spoke English; people spoke Spanish. So imagine my delight when a few years later, after I had moved to Toronto, a friend took me to a matinee at the Runnymede. We sat in this palatial triumph of 1920s "Atmosphere" décor, waiting breathlessly for the stars on the ceiling to dim, and the curtain to go up. The 20th Century Fox searchlights would shine triumphantly. And on to the silvery screen came Betty Grable, platinum blonde with million dollar legs. And speaking in English! Now that's acting, I thought.

I have subsequently revised my idolatry of Betty Grable, but I will never forget the magic of sitting under the stars every Saturday matinee in that fantasy palace. Thank God, Chapters has come along and restored it. When I go in today, I always take a moment, look up at the artificial sky, close my eyes, and for a brief moment, I can see Betty and me dancing and singing and saving the show.

A sign found on the Runnymede projector, when the theatre was converted into a book store, had the bitter-sweet message: TURN OUT THE STARS BEFORE LEAVING!

Hon. John Roberts

When I was a boy growing up in Toronto during the war, our neighbourhood movie theatre just around the corner was the Radio City, now replaced by a high rise apartment building. But, my friends and I usually ignored the Radio City, almost every Saturday afternoon, to walk a few blocks away to the Village Theatre on Spadina Road, on the ritzy outskirts of Forest Hill.

When one entered the Village Theatre, one found an airy rectangular hall. At each side of the screen were two large exit doorways that the architect had decorated with balustrade galleries. Each of theses was topped with the bust of a man, dimly illuminated from behind, leaning over the parapet and, I imagined, staring out towards the assembled audience. There seemed to be something hostile and rather forbidding about their posture. Their countenances, which, of course, could not be seen, I imagined to be certainly somewhat sinister. I knew that these figures were not real but part of the decoration, yet for me the distinction between reality and imagination, which never developed strangely, was even less clearly defined then than it became later in life, and I became obsessed by these figures. Why did they never move? Who were they? Why were they there?

I should mention that those of us that went to these matinees did so, not as passive spectators but equipped for participation. We always arrived with our cap guns strapped on so that we could aid the good guys, by blazing away at the bad guys on the screen, a little like the current theatre goers who go to 'The Sound of Music' to join in and sing along with the action. The matinees were very well attended and as we fired away there should have been a cacophony of "bang, bang, bang" as the caps in our pistols exploded. But this was wartime and the gunpowder to make toy pistol caps was needed for lethal weapons, and so our blazing gunfire ended up being an anemic "click, click, click". But we didn't care. We were intoxicated with the essential and exciting task of helping our screen pal against his enemies. To make doubly sure that he wasn't ambushed from the side I used to shoot at those two sphinx-like figures leaning over the balustrades. They weren't going to hurt our guy if I could help it.

Somehow that all seems long ago, and yet only yesterday. The Village Theatre has long since been converted to other purposes and is, if memory correctly serves, a cleaning establishment. I walk by it sometimes. And I always wonder if somewhere shrouded in the back those two figures are still there, hunched over their balconies, staring straight to the front, waiting for the audiences that now never come.

John MacFarlane, editor

I can't recall his name, or even what he looked like, except that he was tall, dark-haired and mustached. And that he always wore a suit, white shirt and tie, which, even in the 1950s, seemed odd on a Saturday morning. But then he was working, whereas for us, 200 or so members of the Odeon Fairlawn Movie Club, this was recreation, the high point of the week: Saturday morning at the Odeon Fairlawn.

Two or three cartoons, a Buck Rogers serial, and the main event, a Western, starring Audie Murphy, Gene Autry, Roy Rogers or—my favourite—Hopalong Cassidy, would be shown.

The tall, dark-haired, mustached man was the manager of the Odeon Fairlawn, on Yonge Street north of Lawrence Avenue. It was newer and larger than the Park, across and down the street (we liked to point out that Park spelled backward was Krap). The Park was okay. Sometimes we'd see a Western there, too. But it didn't have a Saturday morning movie club, just for kids—and, oh, by the way, when it was your birthday you got in free. Anyway, the manager of the Odeon Fairlawn always introduced the movies, like the program director at a film festival. I must have understood that he didn't actually *know* Hopalong Cassidy, but he was closer to him than I was ever likely to be, and standing there in front of the movie screen he seemed almost as powerful. I blush now to admit it, but the manager of the Odeon Fairlawn was one of my childhood heroes.

At a party 30 years later I spotted him across the room. He was as tall as I remembered him, still dark, and still mustached. In fact, he hadn't changed much at all. I, on the other hand, had finished school, gone to university, started a career, married and had children. Hopalong Cassidy would still have been my favourite cowboy, but practically everything else in my life had changed. And him? Was he still managing the Odeon Fairlawn? It seemed unlikely. But then what? I knew it was the wrong thing to do, but I couldn't help myself. I crossed the room, introduced myself and told him that all those years ago I'd been a member of the Odeon Fairlawn Movie Club. He smiled politely and looked at me with—what was it? Embarrassment? I couldn't tell, but for the first time it occurred to me that for the manager of the Odeon Fairlawn those Saturday mornings I remembered so fondly might actually have been a chore, that hauling himself out of bed to show movies to a bunch of noisy kids might, in fact, have been something of a low point. He didn't offer his name, and I never saw him again.

Gerald Pratley, film historian

I arrived in Toronto in 1946 as a young man; therefore, I have no boyhood memories of the city's many wonderful old cinemas, scattered along the thoroughfares, or the neighbourhood theatres. These always seemed to be around the corner from where friends and families lived. They had the most marvelous names, from the Prince of Wales to the Roxy, the Runnymede and the Royal.

In 1948, I was fortunate to become the CBC's film reviewer, which meant that I had to go to those theatres showing the films that I was expected to see. I did not then have my favourite movie house to attend week after week; I went to almost all of them at one time or another.

However, during the immediate years following, I did become fond of three theatres that played a large part in my future life as a cinephile. These were the Radio City at Bathurst and St. Clair, the Studio at College and Manning, and the International Cinema at Yonge and Manor. All are gone, together with most of the others.

The reason why these three came into my life, apart from showing films that I wanted to see, is because they introduced me to the exhibition side of the film. This was to play an important part in my later life, as a critic, film programmer and teacher.

At first, I worked with Bob and Lionel Lester at the Studio, bringing in some of the first 'foreign' films, as we called them then. At the Radio City, we began some of the first showings from Ottawa's National Film Theatre. The International, I believe, was where Olivier's 'Henry V' was shown, as well as many other British films. Film society screenings were later held here, also.

And so I remember those three cinemas, intimate, pleasing, warm and inviting, creating feelings of anticipation for what we had come to see, and to meet friends and fellow enthusiasts for company and conversation. I shouldn't forget the crockery, knives and forks, and Foto-Nite. I'll trade in the megaplexes to return to them all. They were wonderful halls of pure magic, romance and nostalgia. R.I.P.

John Sebert, photographer

After years of trucking all the way to the Esquire Theatre at Bloor and Durie Streets, we finally got our own theatre in the Kingsway. It was quite modern for 1940, with a glassed-in balcony "crying room" for moms and babies. What I remember, even more than the movies shown, was how my pals and I would sneak in. We would pool our resources (15 cents, I think) and buy a ticket for one of us. He would then enter the theatre and take a seat in the front row. At a particularly dark moment in the picture show, he would slip through one of the curtained exits, which were on either side of the screen, and unlock the fire exit door. The rest of us would then creep in and, for some reason, crawl on our hands and knees across the theatre behind the screen to enter the auditorium on the far side. I will never forget looking up, petrified, as this huge image flashed over our heads as we crept past the blaring speakers. It was very surrealistic. Oh, yes! We were usually caught and thrown out.

Save Our Theatres

This is not a Toronto theatre, but is an excellent example of what can be accomplished when a community gets behind a " Save Our Theatre" project. Historically interesting, the Capitol, in Port Hope, Ontario, was designed by architect Murray Brown in 1930, as an Atmospheric theatre. It features an interior resembling a Tudor village, with clouds rolling by on the ceiling. The Capitol was saved and restored to its Atmospheric capabilities (incidentally only one of two remaining in all of Canada) by the community of Port Hope. It is now in full time use as a performing arts venue, and movie theatre.

Archives of Ontario: RG 56-11-4.46

Capitol (1940) *14 Queen St., west side, Port Hope*

The End